ENHANCING ADULT LITERACY

A POLICY GUIDE

by
Jack A. Brizius
Susan E. Foster

The Council of State Policy & Planning Agencies
Hall of the States
400 North Capitol, Room 291
Washington, D.C., 20001

Funding support for this publication was provided by a grant from the John D. and Catherine T. MacArthur Foundation. While many state policy officials and experts in the field of literacy have contributed to the production of this paper, the statements, findings, conclusions, and recommendations are solely those of the authors.

Council of State Policy & Planning Agencies

Hall of the States
400 North Capitol Street, Suite 291
Washington, D.C. 20001

James M. Souby
Executive Director

Barbara R. Dyer
Project Director

Judith K. Chynoweth
Editor

TABLE OF CONTENTS

iii

TABLE OF CONTENTS, Cont.

TABLE OF CONTENTS, Cont.

FOREWORD

ENHANCING ADULT LITERACY: A PUBLIC POLICY GUIDE is a valuable tool for governors and their staffs as they seek to enhance adult literacy. This book offers practical guidance in two areas critical to effective action: it clarifies definitions of "literacy" and "illiteracy" and provides a framework for designing gubernatorial policy and choosing strategies. The guide also presents a cogent discussion of the role of state government and the role of the governor in solving problems arising from low levels of literacy.

As a governor, I have a tremendous sense of responsibility to help people find employment; but as we attempt to create more economic opportunities for productive citizens, we encounter obstacles between people and opportunities. Funtional illiteracy is perhaps the most basic barrier to productive employment.

Those of us who have reviewed this problem in our states have discovered that twenty to forty percent of young adults drop out of high school before graduation; many citizens cannot read, write and compute beyond a fourth grade level; and many of those who do have basic skills cannot adjust successfully to new work environments. There is also a growing awareness that sixty to seventy percent of prison inmates and welfare recipients may not read, write, or compute well enough to get and keep a job.

Today the concept of literacy encompasses reasoning and problem-solving skills that enable individuals to learn new tasks and to adapt to changing situations. The lack of these skills continues to be a threat to the social and economic health of the United States. If America is to be competitive in the global economy, and if states are to be full participants in that economy, workers must have the literacy skills needed to perform the tasks that changing technology demands.

The CSPA Policy Guide was prepared to support the CSPA STATE POLICY ACADEMY ON   INCREASING LITERACY FOR JOBS AND PRODUCTIVITY. Missouri is proud to be the lead state in this literacy partnership involving ten states, several federal agencies, and the National Governors' Association.

I am certain the Council of State Policy and Planning Agencies has produced a policy guide worthy of your review and one that will prove useful as you address the literacy challenge in your state.

Governor John Ashcroft
Missouri

ACKNOWLEDGMENTS

The contributions of many individuals and organizations made this work possible. In particular, we would like to thank Pete Gerber of the MacAuthur Foundation for his support and guidance, and Tom Duncan who worked with us on behalf of Governor Ashcroft. Judy Chynoweth and Barbara Dyer of the Council of State Policy & Planning Agencies provided considerable help in reviewing drafts of this publication and in linking this work to the policy academies on increasing literacy for jobs and productivity. The support of Jim Souby, Executive Director for the Council, was important as well. The works of David Harman, Irwin Kirsch, and Larry Mikulecky served as invaluable guidance in the formulation of our ideas for this volume. Nancy Ginn-Helme completed a survey of state gubernatorial initiatives in adult literacy which was also a useful resource. We would also particularly like to thank a group of individuals who served tirelessly as reviewers and advisers for the preparation of this volume: Sharon Darling, literacy consultant; Lloyd Feldman and Gerri Fiala of the U.S. Department of Labor; Evelyn Ganzglass of the National Governors' Association; Jean Hammick, literacy consultant; and Karl Haigler and Benita Sommerfield of the U.S. Department of Education.

CHAPTER 1

ILLITERACY, LITERACY, AND PUBLIC POLICY

Item: Ford Motor Company decided to make an all-out effort to improve manufacturing in Ypsilanti, Michigan, by training the entire workforce in statistical process controls. The program was a bust. Half the group lacked sufficient literacy skills to understand the material. The next step — a reading program for employees.

Item: General Electric's new plastics plant in Lowndes County, Alabama, employs state-of-the-art technology and highly skilled people. GE's decision to open a plant in Lowndes is a plus for the community, but the company cannot rely on the community for its current or future labor force. Lowndes residents have poor reading and math skills and the performance of students in public schools is very poor. Working together, community and GE leaders established a broad-based program to improve math, science, and engineering skills of students. The hope is that the next generation of engineers hired will be Lowndes residents.

Item: In Boston, a welfare mother was turned down when she applied for an employment and training program, touted by the Governor as the best way to move from welfare to work. Her reading and math skills were so low that the training program could not accept her. The Governor decided that his newly formed Literacy Corps would make a top priority of helping welfare women get basic literacy skills.

These examples are not unique. They reflect a pervasive literacy problem which affects the health of the economy and the future of millions of Americans. While the White House estimates that there are 26 million "functionally illiterate" adults in America, no one really knows how many adults do not have adequate reading, writing, and communications skills. More and more people do know, however, that their skills are inadequate for the job market. Increasing numbers of companies, striving to improve productivity and quality by using more sophisticated technology, are having difficulty fitting employees to company needs. Employers and employees alike are discovering that too many adults in America cannot read, write, compute, communicate, or solve problems well enough.

America's governors believe that solving the problem of adult literacy is crucial to the economic future of their states. Adult literacy is more than a temporary labor supply and demand issue. The health of an economy in transition depends on the skills and adaptability of the labor force. Adult literacy is essential to the future adaptability of the labor force and to the ability of the economy to become more productive and competitive. Missouri's Governor John Ashcroft, Chairman of the National Governors' Association's Task Force on Adult Literacy, has recognized that "the most basic barrier to productive employment any person can face is functional illiteracy". He has called for "a reexamination of the entire literacy delivery system" in the states.[1] The governors collectively are focusing determined attention upon the issue of adult literacy as part of their far-reaching campaign to improve productivity and "Make America Work."

To make America work more productively and to ensure the health of the economy, state leaders are addressing the close connection between literacy, jobs, and productivity. As the U.S. economy undergoes a transition from production processes based on repetitive tasks to those based on the application of significant and new technology, a new kind of labor force will be required. The success of the economy depends on the literacy and reasoning skills of the labor force. Assistant Secretary of Labor Roger Semerad noted recently,

> In the new technology-driven economy, many new and existing jobs will require higher levels of analytical and communications skills; the level of literacy required will continue to rise beyond mere reading and writing ability; and the rapid turnover and change of industries and firms will transform the work culture of Americans, with many workers changing jobs five or six times during their work lives.[2]

The costs of addressing the issue of adult literacy are great, but the consequences of ignoring the needs of millions of Americans for improved basic skills are even greater. Corporate America already spends over $30 billion for education and training of current employees. Government spends many billions more on elementary and secondary education, higher education, and job training. With all this investment, however, the lack of functional literacy among millions of adults is costing the national economy billions of dollars in productivity losses, lowered quality, and lost opportunities for people to move up into more skilled jobs.

In response to this problem, many organizations have developed programs aimed at improving literacy levels for particular segments of the population. Corporations sponsor special classes designed to improve the skills of their employees. Government agencies provide literacy training through welfare and jobs programs and prisons. Community colleges and schools offer adult basic education classes, and volunteers work with individuals in attempts to improve their reading skills. All of these programs are offered with different goals and approaches to instruction. No one really knows how much these programs improve literacy skills, but available evidence suggests that progress is slow and attrition is very high. Two examples illustrate this point:

> An adult basic education class has convened at a local community college facility for its eighth session. There are twelve people in the class – eight fewer than at the start of the course. Three participants are attending their second year of the same course, even though they were graduated from the program. Many of the participants are unemployed welfare recipients; several arrive directly after work. The teacher is a professional adult educator. Progress is slow, almost imperceptible. The teacher tries new ways to encourage her students, but attendance remains sporadic, the dropout rate remains high, and it appears that progress is excruciatingly slow.[3]

> In St. Louis a volunteer literacy teacher has arrived for her weekly session with a single mother of three. The volunteer has attended a brief, two-day training session, during which she was instructed in the use of various materials and provided some pointers regarding various aspects of her new avocation. Their session lasts an hour and a half. Progress is very slow and the volunteer has become frustrated by her seeming inability to teach her charge how to read. Five months after beginning her work, the volunteer instructor takes a vacation. When she returns, she discovers that her student has moved and no one knows how to reach her.[4]

Addressing the issue of adult literacy requires political leadership and leadership requires a clear understanding of literacy issues. Governors are beginning to ask: What is literacy? What skills are needed for what purposes? How many people lack needed skills? How effective are our existing programs? Who should be doing what to ameliorate the problem? Governors are concerned because of the enormous social and economic costs associated with poor literacy skills, and because states – through their direct investment in education, training, reducing dependency, and economic development – are central players. But literacy is not an issue for the states alone. While states can contribute leadership, provide direction, and offer resources, all sectors must combine forces if the problem is to be solved.

This policy guide is designed to assist governors and state leaders in analyzing the issue of adult literacy and in proposing specific policy strategies for dealing with this significant national problem. In its approach to the issue, the guide is based upon several assumptions about adult literacy and its importance to the health of the economy and the society:

A strong economy requires an educated, well-trained, and adaptable labor force. The level of education and skills among workers is the primary determinant of long-term economic health. More important than taxation, the regulatory environment, or the "business climate," the skills of the labor force are essential both for attracting new industry and for the growth of new and existing firms within a state's boundaries. Peter Drucker emphasizes:

> The basic factor in an economy's development must be the rate of 'brain formation'— the rate at which a country produces people with imagination and vision, education, theoretical and analytical skills.[5]

Economic development and the health of a state or national economy "depends on the rate at which we accumulate human

5

capital: the knowledge and skills that people accumulate through education, training, and/or experience that enable them to supply valuable productive service to others."[6] A state with large numbers of workers who cannot perform the basic functions of reading, writing, and mathematics will have difficulty in growing economically in an increasingly competitive world economy.

Enhancing adult literacy will take more than just improvements in public elementary and secondary education. Adult literacy cannot be ensured purely by reforming and improving the public schools. About 70 percent of the labor force in the year 2000 has already left school. If economic prospects are to be improved through upgrading the skills of the labor force, literacy must be addressed among today's adults. In the future, improvements in public education may reduce the need for adult education, but it is equally likely that immigration and the changing requirements of the labor market will require more training of adults in different kinds of "literacy" than today.

Improving the educational performance of the next generation will require literacy improvements among their parents. In spite of the attractive American myth of the self-taught, ambitious youngster who overcomes his or her parent's illiteracy and poverty to succeed, the reality is that if parents are not literate, their children start far behind and may never catch up. Education begins long before kindergarten.

Though we are asking the school system to perform more effectively, the preparedness of children entering school is dropping, especially among poor, single-parent families. Jonathan Kozol points out that the children of nonreaders could be a "pedagogic time bomb" threatening to destroy any advances that education reform policies may otherwise bring.

Illiterate parents have no way to give their children pre-school preparation which enables them to profit fully from a good school or —in the more common case—which will protect those children, by the learning that takes place at home, against the dangers of the worst schools.[7]

If we can teach parents the skills they need to be literate in today's society, they will have a better chance of helping their children learn these same skills. More important, if we can instill an interest in learning, parents will be able to help their children learn how to learn. Literacy is a cultural and family value as well as a set of skills.

Improving literacy in the culture of American life today requires a shift in values. Literacy is not a highly valued commodity in today's mass media. Movies and TV shows rarely show people reading; teenagers graduate from high school without basic skills; few adults spend much time reading to their children or helping them learn how to solve problems. If adults are encouraged to value literacy, this value will be passed on to their children and spread throughout the community. Efforts to enhance the literacy of parents and change the basic values about literacy in our society may be as important as the reform of schooling itself.

Efforts to reduce economic dependency and reduce crime cannot succeed without upgrading the educational levels of many on welfare, in prison, or otherwise dependent. While it is unlikely that the elimination of illiteracy would automatically decrease welfare dependency or crime, it is safe to assume that individuals who are not literate will have a harder time getting off welfare or staying away from crime. That poverty and levels of literacy are associated is indisputable. David Harman notes that

7

poverty, disadvantage, low self-esteem, inability to compete successfully in a competitive society, and the impact of disadvantage on children are all nonquantifiable social costs. Illiteracy is clearly one of the attributes of these situations and its elimination would contribute to their alleviation. Literacy, on its own, however, cannot solve these problems.[8]

Solving literacy problems may be a precondition for attacking other social ills. For poor people and minorities, addressing the literacy issue may be of crucial importance. "For many of the poor, for many minorities, and for those with minimal schooling, literacy needs are only one of a complex of problems, and no single program will solve them all. But improvement of literacy skills is a necessary step for eventually allowing every American to participate fully in society."[9]

Literacy is required to exercise fully the rights of citizenship. Broader questions involving literacy and citizenship, participation in the political process, and the communities within the states also motivate the governors to become concerned about literacy. The fact that perhaps as high as 40 percent of Americans do not read a daily newspaper,[10] for example, affects political participation, information gathering, and the making of public policy in the states and nation. If large numbers of people cannot read, write, and calculate, the ability of the people to make informed political choices is threatened. As state and local officials take on more responsibilities regarding domestic issues, the questions of citizenship and literacy become increasingly important to governors.

America, the melting pot, is a nation of immigrants who seek opportunity and eventually assimilate into the economic and social mainstream. In recent years, however, enclaves of non-

English-speaking communities, and those for whom English is a second language, have developed in isolation from the mainstream of American life. People in these enclaves do not vote or otherwise participate in the democratic process; they may not share the same drive to assimilate into American society as earlier immigrant groups have. For many of them, government is at best irrelevant, at worst a source of fear. To prevent an increasing disaffection of large groups of persons from the mainstream of the American economic and political system, a bridge connecting cultures, values, goals, and opportunities must be fashioned. This bridge is literacy.

Governors are concerned about literacy for both humanistic and economic reasons. Illiteracy is a human tragedy. Literacy is the first link in the chain between education, job skills, labor force adaptability, and economic growth. Literacy is an essential prerequisite for economic advancement and competitiveness in a global economy. Because of the demographic changes which portend slower growth in the labor force, policymakers must strive to upgrade the skills of today's workers and provide for a better education for the workers of tomorrow. To meet the current and increasing demands for an educated, well-trained and productive labor force, governors recognize the need to take significant steps to enhance adult literacy.

This policy guide is intended to help state officials design strategic policies for enhancing adult literacy. It addresses questions that governors are likely to ask as the policymaking process unfolds. Chapter Two discusses the definitional and measurement issues involved in giving the governor a clear picture of the adult literacy problem in a state. An approach to the adult literacy issue that targets limited resources and relates literacy policy to broad state goals is offered in Chapter Three. Chapter Four assesses the use of a wide range of state powers and gubernatorial influence for addressing the problem. The "state of the art" in literacy enhancement programs is reviewed in Chapter Five, which also offers guidelines for policy and program development. Chapter Six discusses the governor's unique role in leading efforts to address literacy and offers a range of policy options for attacking the problem. Chapter Seven concludes with a summary of the central issues discussed in the policy guide and a brief summary of strategic aproaches to implementing adult literacy policy.

Chapter 1 Notes

1. Governor John Ashcroft, *Governors' Bulletin* (Washington, D.C.: National Governors' Association, April 6, 1987).

2. Remarks by Roger D. Semerad, Assistant Secretary of Labor at "Workforce 2000" Briefing, Management 21, (Nashville, Tennessee, October 22, 1986).

3. David Harman, *Illiteracy: A National Dilemna* (New York: The Cambridge Book Company, 1987), 80 - 82.

4. Ibid, 83 - 85.

5. Peter Drucker, *Management* (London: Pan Books, 1979), 63.

6. Roger Vaughn, Robert Pollard, Barbara Dyer, *Wealth of States* (Washington, D.C.: Council of State Policy and Planning Agencies, 1985), 85.

7. Jonathan Kozol, *Illiterate America* (Garden City, New York: Anchor Press/ Doubleday, 1985), 59.

8. David Harman, *Turning Illiteracy Around: An Agenda for National Action* (New York: Business Council for Effective Literacy, 1985), 11.

9. Richard L Venezky, et. al., *The Subtle Danger* (Princeton, New Jersey: Educational Testing Service, 1987), 8.

10. Jonathan Kozol, *Illiterate America* (Garden City, New York: Anchor Press/ Doubleday, 1985), 33.

CHAPTER 2

DEFINING AND MEASURING LITERACY

INTRODUCTION

The level of literacy necessary in any society is determined by the requirements for economic and social functioning. The definition of literacy must, therefore, adapt to economic and cultural change. Simple and seemingly absolute definitions of literacy are not appropriate to changing social and economic realities.

For a governor and his or her staff, definitional debates may be intellectually stimulating; but, unless they are useful to policy development, they are meaningless exercises. There are two important reasons for exploring the definitions of literacy. First, unless policymakers relate literacy to the current cultural and economic context of their states, they cannot make crucial judgments that will link literacy enhancement to other important policy goals. Second, policymakers require a clear definition of literacy in order to measure the extent of the adult literacy problem in each state.

The purpose of this chapter is to explore a continuum of definitions of literacy so that a governor and his or her staff can choose the definition that makes the most sense in their state's unique policy environment. In addition, the definitions help to tie numbers to identifiable points on the literacy continuum. This will enable state officials to estimate the numbers of persons associated with various levels of literacy in their states. The chapter continues with a discussion of three methodological approaches to estimating literacy, based on selected definitions, and concludes with some practical ways of making these estimates as realistic as possible as governors begin to develop policies concerning adult literacy.

LITERACY AND ILLITERACY: THE RECEDING DEFINITIONAL HORIZON

Virtually all students of adult literacy agree that "literacy" and "illiteracy" are relative concepts, not very useful apart from the cultural, social, and economic context in which they are derived. Throughout much of U.S. history, they point out, "literacy" was defined as being able to sign one's name. In most of the third world, "literacy" is defined at a level of reading and writing that most Americans would judge "illiterate." While most would agree that anyone who cannot read or write his name is "illiterate", a common definition of a "literate" person is difficult to achieve without defining the social context and the expectations placed on an individual.

David Harman has summed up the difficulty in defining "literacy":

> The attempt to define literacy is like a walk to the horizon: as one walks toward it, it continuously recedes. Similarly, as groups of people achieve the skills formerly defined as literacy, altered circumstances often render definitions obsolete. New definitions replace the old ones as new goals are set. People considered literate by a previous yardstick are now regarded as illiterate.[1]

In addition to being relative to the time and culture, literacy and illiteracy are not conditions that can be diagnosed like a disease or readily measured. Harman points out how the disease analogy is flawed.

> Illiteracy is not a simple "disease" — it is a complicated manifestation of multiple causes and is deeply rooted in both culture and social dynamic. Literacy is not the simple ability to read and write — it is a highly complex concept that derives its definition from different conditions among different groups at different times.[2]

Yet the political dynamic of state policymaking encourages policymakers to speak in terms of "eliminating" and "combatting" illiteracy much as if illiteracy were a disease. Governors and other policymakers must recognize that literacy and illiteracy are not discrete conditions, but at the same time they must be able to define the extent of the problem confronting their states. In order to communicate both the reality of the problem and the differing definitions of literacy, it may be most useful to think of a continuum of definitions, a spectrum of skills against which everyone's "literacy" can be measured.

LITERACY: A CONTINUUM OF DEFINITIONS

According to the United Nations, "a person is literate who can with understanding both read and write a short, simple statement on his everyday life."[3] Despite the difficulty in defining literacy and illiteracy, at least seven other definitions have been put forward in the United States. These definitions can be used by state policymakers as a starting point in establishing where the state's adults lie on the literacy continuum. These definitions of literacy can be arrayed in an

13

order ranging from the most exacting (and least inclusive) to the least exacting (and therefore most inclusive):

Number of Years of Schooling and Ability to Read. Persons are illiterate who are over fourteen years of age with less than a sixth grade education and are unable to read or write English at all or are unable to read or write a language other than English that was spoken at home. This definition was established in a study in 1979. Based on this definition, the Census Bureau estimated in 1985 that the 1980 illiteracy rate was less than one-half of one percent, or about 900,000 adults.[4]

Years of Schooling. For many years, the Census Bureau has defined literacy as the completion of six or more years of school. Those completing less than six years of school were assumed to be illiterate. In 1982, about 5.2 million adults had completed less than six years of school.[5]

National Assessment of Educational Progress (NAEP). "Using printed and written information to function in society, to achieve one's goals, and to develop one's knowledge and potential." This definition was the basis for the development of a continuum of literacy skills measured on a scale of 150 to 500. Three areas — prose literacy, document literacy, and quantitative literacy — were measured among young adults aged twenty-one to twenty-five in 1986. The results of the NAEP study are discussed later in this chapter. Among all levels, the NAEP found that less than 1 percent of young adults scored at the lowest level (150) and that less than 5 percent scored at less than the 200 level of competence. At higher levels, the percentages who could not perform increased markedly.[6]

English Language Proficiency. In an analysis conducted by the Department of Education based on a Census study of

English language proficiency, persons considered illiterate were those who could not answer twenty of twenty-six questions on a simple written test in which individuals were asked to identify key words and phrases and match them to four alternatives. Analysts chose their cut-off point in applying the results of the English Language Proficiency Study (ELPS) so that it would reflect approximately a fourth grade reading level. Based on the ELPS conducted in the fall of 1982, the Department of Education found that nationwide about 13 percent of adults were "illiterate."[7]

Conventional and Functional Literacy. In 1979, Harman and Hunter proposed the most widely used definitions of literacy. These include conventional literacy; defined as "the ability to read, write, and comprehend texts on familiar subjects and to understand whatever signs, labels, instructions, directions, etc., are necessary to get along within one's environment," and functional literacy; defined as "the possession of skills perceived as necessary by particular persons or groups to fulfill their own self-determined objectives as family and community members, citizens, consumers, job holders and members of social, religious, or other associations of their choosing. This includes the ability to obtain information they want and to use that information for their own and another's well-being. This also includes:

- Ability to read and write adequately to satisfy the requirements they set for themselves as being important in their own lives;
- Ability to deal positively with demands made on them by society; and,
- Ability to solve problems they face in their daily lives."[8]

15

Hunter and Harman's definition of functional literacy expands the boundaries of what most people define as simple literacy. He notes that "functional literacy, even more than mechanical reading and writing skills, is a relative set of capabilities. It can only derive its real definition from actual conditions pertaining in a particular situation and does not lend itself to generalization."[9]

This definition of functional literacy has not been used to measure specific numbers of people who are functionally literate or illiterate. Rather, the Hunter and Harman definitions have been used to stress the relative nature of literacy and the concept of literacy as a social value.

Adult Performance Level (APL) Definitions. In the Adult Performance Level study published in 1975, three levels of "adult functional competency" were established, based on levels of adult success measured by income, job status, and education.

The APL study correlated these three levels of adult functional "success" with results of a series of tests of reading, writing, and computational capabilities. This study (discussed in greater detail later in this chapter) found that 20 percent of the adult population functioned "with difficulty" and another 34 percent were merely "functional" (as opposed to "proficient").[10]

Completion of High School. Robinson and others have suggested that a definition of "functional literacy" might be the completion of high school.[11] By this definition, slightly less than 34 percent of adults aged twenty-five and older were functionally illiterate in 1980. Because high school graduation rates are higher now than in the past, this percentage should have slightly decreased by 1987.

In addition to these definitions of literacy and illiteracy, attempts have been made to attempt to define "occupational literacy." Broadly speaking, occupational literacy is defined as a set of skills necessary to perform a specific job or type of job. Although the minimum levels of literacy for many occupations have been defined, no single standard of "occupational literacy" can be applied.[12] Since the issue of "occupational literacy" is at the heart of the governors' concern about adult literacy, state officials may want to try to work with employers, unions, and other groups to translate definitions of occupational literacy into measures that can be used to define literacy more broadly. When employers complain about the level of literacy of the work force, they should provide more information concerning the types of "occupational literacy' that they require.

As this brief listing indicates, definitions are highly sub-jective, depending upon the perceptions of those defining the terms— perceptions of what it means to function in society, hold a job, educate children, and participate in community life. Although most people would not readily define "literacy" or even "functional literacy" as requiring a high school education, for example, there are many who believe that the economic future of the nation may require such a definition. Similarly, few would suggest that the ability to sign one's name is a guarantee of literacy, but we know that in times past this definition was nearly universal.

Literacy and illiteracy are not absolute conditions but are part of a continuum of skills. Viewed from this perspective, the problems associated with defining literacy and illiteracy are manage-able. When state policymakers look at definitions of literacy they should be examining a continuum of reading, writing, math, and communications skills, not trying to determine what the cut-off point for "literacy" or "illiteracy"may be.

As the authors of *The Subtle Danger* observe,

> Literacy is not an all-or-nothing state, like smallpox or pregnancy. It is instead a continuum of skills that are acquired both in and outside formal schooling and that relate directly to the ability to function within society.[13]

Recognizing that all individuals or groups of adults fall somewhere on the continuum of literacy, the task of the policymaker is not to define literacy, but to decide where to put resources to help some people move along the literacy continuum and to judge how far it is necessary for people to move so that other goals, such as creating jobs or improving productivity, can be met.

MEASURING LITERACY

Using these definitions of literacy, the illiteracy rate in the United States can be said to be as low as .5 percent or as high as about 50 percent of adult Americans. Even for a governor or state policymaker used to making judgments based on incomplete information, this is an astonishing range. Depending on one's definition, adult literacy is either a massive problem in America or no problem at all. By looking at the estimates associated with each of these definitions, perhaps we can cut through the thicket of definitional and measurement problems and come to some reasonable conclusions about the numbers of people associated with various levels of literacy in our states.

A practical approach to this problem is used frequently by political executives who constantly deal with competing claims among interest groups, legislators, and staff:

> *Throw out the extreme estimates and focus on the "reasonable middle." Examine the middle ground carefully for policy implications. Test all of these assumptions with experience in state programs and everyday life.*

This approach is justifiable on the grounds of sheer practicality and basic common sense. If the lack of literacy skills is only a problem for .5 percent of the population, there are many other pressing social problems that should occupy the time and energy of policymakers. Moreover, a low estimate does not correlate with growing concern about the problem, increasingly expressed by members of the business community and labor. If, on the other hand, a definition that encompasses half the population is used, policymakers will dismiss the relevance of the definition because it simply does not correspond to their own experience.

This policy guide recommends that policymakers take this practical approach to estimating the extent of adult illiteracy or the need for additional literacy skills. Below are four methods of estimating adult literacy and illiteracy, based on different approaches to the definitional problem. These four methods are:

- Estimating literacy rates through use of the ELPS approach;
- Estimating literacy rates through the NAEP approach;
- Estimating literacy rates through application of the APL data; and,
- Estimating literacy rates through school grade-level completion information.

For governors concerned with developing an adult literacy strategy, each of these approaches has strengths and weaknesses. A more complete discussion of each of these methods follows.

The ELPS Approach

The approach taken by the Census in its English Language Proficiency survey focused entirely on reading and language abilities. In a test comprising twenty-six very simple questions, a national sample of 3,400 persons aged twenty and over was asked to read short sentences and then answer multiple choice questions or fill in blanks with the appropriate word relating to the sentence. An example of the test illustrates how basic the questions were. Test takers were asked to "choose the answer that means the same as the word or phrase with a line under it."

> Question 6: "This is to notify you that your application for assistance
> has been <u>denied</u>."
> a. turned down
> b. reviewed
> c. accepted
> d. mailed out

Other sections of the test asked people to fill in blanks:

> "Soon, you'll receive a new medical services program identification card. It will replace all other medical _____."
> a. bills
> b. cards
> c. types
> d. checks

In this analysis of the Census data, the Department of Education selected a "cutoff point" — a score of twenty or above — as defining literacy in English. The cutoff point related to common sense notions about the relationship between literacy and school completion. The study notes, "specifically, among native English speakers, less than 1 percent of those completing some college scored below 20, in contrast to a failure rate of more than 50 percent for those with fewer than 6 years of school."[14]

To generalize the results of the test to the population as a whole, the study examined characteristics of the "literate" and "non-literate" portions of the sample. The analysis looked at factors that could be found only in the 1980 census. It found strong correlations with test performance for the following six factors: age, nativity, recency of immigration for non-natives, race, poverty status, amount of schooling, and reported English-speaking ability of persons who used a non-English language at home. Regression coefficients were estimated for each of these variables and then applied to the population with the above "risk factors" in each state to develop state-by-state estimates of literacy. For example, the strongest correlation to "illiteracy" was found for the characteristic "persons age 25+ with 0-4 years of school," not a surprising result. Since the 1980 Census revealed the number in each state with that characteristic, the study applied the regression coefficient to state-by-state data to arrive at a number of these persons who would be expected to be "illiterate"(not score twenty on the ELPS test).

By applying coefficients for all the risk factors and adding up the at risk population, the study arrived at estimates of the total number of adults "at risk" of illiteracy in each state. The study worked from the characteristics of the test sample back to estimates of illiteracy in each state. The assumption was that if most blacks with less than six years of schooling who took the test could not pass it, for example, most blacks with less than six years of schooling in Louisiana were similarly "illiterate."

The results of the study showed that about 13 percent of the U.S. adult population were likely to be "illiterate". The study estimated that about 18.7 million adults were "illiterate" by this definition in 1982. This represents about 3.5 times the number estimated to have completed less than six years of school.

State estimates ranged from a low of 6 percent in Utah to a high of 16 percent in Louisiana, Mississippi, and Texas. As one would expect, states with high percentages of minority populations and high rates of poverty and immigration also had the largest percentages of people at risk of low levels of literacy. An analysis of other characteristics of those classified as illiterate revealed a number of interesting conclusions:

(1) Of all the adults likely to be illiterate,
- over forty percent lived in central cities of metropolitan areas, while only eight percent lived in rural areas;
- thirty-seven percent of illiterate adults spoke a non-English language at home; and,
- forty-four percent were aged fifty and older; fifty-six percent were under age fifty.

(2) Among native English speakers likely to be illiterate,
- seventy percent did not finish high school;
- forty-two percent had no earnings in the previous year; and,
- thirty-five percent were in their twenties and thirties.

(3) Among illiterate adults who used a non-English language,
- eighty-two percent were born outside the United States; and,
- twenty-one percent had entered the U.S. within the previous six years.

Although the methodology of the study may seem complex, state-by-state results seems to conform to common sense. In states with large immigrant populations, low levels of literacy present a bigger problem than in states where the population has been stable for many years. States with a tradition of low levels of school completion have more adults with low levels of literacy skills than those with high rates of high school graduation or school completion.

Residents of poor states suffer from lower levels of literacy than those from relatively wealthy ones, except where wealthy states have attracted large numbers of recent immigrants. This picture of the "illiterate" population presented by the Department of Education's analysis of the ELPS data will help state policymakers develop their own baseline estimates of literacy within their states.

If one is primarily interested in developing estimates of illiteracy among the work force, the ELPS study by the Department of Education provides at least some hints about the incidence of illiteracy among those likely to be in the labor force. About two-thirds of those defined as illiterate in the ELPS study were in the labor force, yet more than half were unemployed. Most of these potential workers had not finished high school. Slightly more than half were under the age of fifty. They were disproportionately black and Hispanic. Many were recent immigrants and most lived in metropolitan areas with large concentrations in central cities.

The ELPS definition of literacy is a relatively narrow one. Literacy was defined as basic English proficiency. It is possible that many of the non-English-speaking people classified by this study as "illiterate" are in fact functionally literate in their own language. In fact, the study estimates that about 14 percent of non-English speakers are literate in their own language, based on their reported education. At the same time, it is also possible that large numbers of those classified as "literate" by the ELPS definition are not functioning well at work or in the community because of other educational deficiencies, such as lack of computational abilities.

The NAEP Study of Literacy Among Young Adults

The Educational Testing Service's National Assessment of Educational Progress has inventoried the literacy skills of young adults across the nation. In the process, the NAEP study has examined many of the definitional problems associated with illiteracy for the entire population. As discussed earlier, the NAEP defines literacy as the ability to use printed information "to function in society, to achieve one's goals, and to develop one's knowledge and potential."[15]

In developing tests to measure levels of literacy among adults aged twenty-one to twenty-five, the NAEP design reflected the fact that literacy is a continuum of skills. As Thomas Sticht wrote in the introduction to the study,

> Conceptually, this study avoids the almost universal tendency to oversimplify the nature of literacy and divide the population into neat categories of 'illiterate,' 'functionally illiterate,' and 'literate.' Rather, it recognizes that people develop a variety of literacy abilities that reflect the social settings in which they interact with printed materials, whether this be the home, community, school or workplace.[16]

The study tested skills in three areas of competency:

> *Prose Literacy:* the knowledge and skills needed to understand and use information from texts that include editorials, news stories, poems and the like;
> *Document Literacy:* the knowledge and skills required to locate and use information contained in job applications or payroll forms, bus schedules, maps, tables, indexes, and so forth; and,
> *Quantitative Literacy:* the knowledge and skills needed to apply arithmetic operations, either alone or sequentially, that are embedded in printed materials, such as balancing a checkbook, figuring out a tip, completing an order form, or determining the amount of interest from a loan advertisement.

In addition, results from the assessment based on each of these scales were presented on a fourth scale. That scale calculated a reading proficiency score that could be compared with previous assessments of reading skills for high school seniors.

Questions in each section of the test were not simple matching or multiple choice questions. Instead, the tests asked young adults to perform tasks simulating those they might encounter in real life: reading a newspaper article for key facts, using a menu, selecting bargains from a food advertisement, or deciphering a bus schedule.

In each of the three areas tested, scales were developed ranging from the simplest to the most difficult. A range of scores from 0 to 500 was possible, although most questions ranged in levels of difficulty from 125 to about 400. In the document literacy section of the test, for example, the least demanding task asked a respondent to write her or his name on the appropriate line of a social security card. A more demanding task (350 level) required the respondent to locate and match six features or categories on a bus schedule. [17]

By constructing tests of young adults' abilities to perform tasks at increasing levels of difficulty, the NAEP study developed a "profile of literacy" instead of a test of absolute "literacy" or "illiteracy." Equally important, the study examined not only the decoding aspects of literacy but also the information-processing tasks required to function in today's society.

The NAEP study drew a nationally representative sample of 3,600 young adults, aged twenty-one to twenty-five, from 40,000 households in the contiguous forty-eight states. Each respondent was interviewed for about ninety minutes, with sixty minutes devoted to the assessment and about thirty minutes to identify background characteristics of the young adult. From this sample, information concerning both the literacy skills of the sample and their racial, ethnic, school completion, and other characteristics was collected.

The conclusion of the study was summarized in *Literacy: Profiles of Young Adults*:

> It is clear from these data that 'illiteracy' is not a major problem for this population. It is also clear, however, that 'literacy' is a problem.[18]

By this statement, the authors reflected the fact that only a very small percentage of the sample of young adults were unable to perform tasks at the lower levels of functioning measured in the assessment. As the level of complexity of the tasks in the assessment rose, however, the performance of the sample dropped off rapidly. Overall, on a scale of 0 to 500 the sample's average performance was 305. The authors report that "most young adults were estimated to be proficient at the tasks represented at the lower end of each scale, and more than half were estimated to have attained moderate levels of proficiency on each of the. . .scales. Nevertheless, relatively few young adults were estimated to have reached levels of proficiencies associated with the most complex and demanding tasks."[19]

An examination of the performance of the entire sample on each of the three scales illustrates both the positive news — that few young adults are absolutely illiterate — and the more troubling finding — that few young adults can deal successfully with more complex tasks:

- At the lowest levels in the assessment, young adults performed relatively well on all three scales. About 96 percent of the sample could perform at the 200 level on the prose, document and quantitative assessments.
- Performance dropped off rapidly, however, as the complexity of the tasks increased. At the 250 level, for example, less than 83 percent performed adequately on

the prose scale, less than 84 percent on the document scale, and less than 85 percent on the quantitative assessment.

- Performance on more complex tasks, the 350 level for example, was low. Only about 21 percent could perform 350 level tasks on the prose scale, 20 percent on the document scale and less than 23 percent on the quantitative scale.

Within the overall sample, an analysis of performance by subgroups reveals similarities in performance at lower levels but large differences at moderate and high levels of performance:[20]

- At least with regard to mean performance, men and women performed essentially equally.
- Black and Hispanic young adults performed significantly less well on all four literacy scales than did whites. This gap was particularly significant at moderate and high levels of performance. The mean scores of whites on the prose, document and quantitative scales was about 315, while blacks scored between 255 and 264 and Hispanics scored between 278 and 287.
- Not surprisingly, the level of educational attainment was positively associated with performance on all the scales. The mean score for prose literacy, for example, was 263 for high school dropouts, 292 for high school graduates, 327 for those with a 2-year post-secondary degree and 343 for college graduates. Interestingly, the study reported that "on average, young adults perform significantly better on the NAEP reading scale than do in-school 17-year-olds. This suggests that further education and participation in society contribute to the improvement in reading skills. [21]

- A strong correlation between dropping out of school and low performance on the literacy scales was evident from the NAEP study. Young adults who had dropped out of school scored 40 to 60 points below the mean in the sample. Particularly affected were young women who had dropped out because of pregnancy, who "were consistently at the very bottom of each literacy-skills distribution."
- Family background was an important predictor of literacy skills. Since family background, especially educational attainment of parents, is associated with school completion and other factors, the influence of family variables on literacy performance was expected. A statistical analysis of the relationship between parental educational attainment and performance on the NAEP assessment revealed that "parents' educational attainment has a substantial influence on the availability of literacy materials in the home, the choice of a college-preparatory curriculum during high school and the ultimate amount of educational attainment achieved by young adults."

The problem of low levels of literacy skills is not so much that young adults have no literacy skills at all but rather that they lack skills that can be applied to more complex tasks. Especially important is the conclusion of the NAEP study that young adults lack problem-solving skills, the very skills that may be most needed in the economy of the future.

The Adult Performance Level (APL) Approach

Perhaps attempting to measure literacy and illiteracy is less relevant to policymaking than is an assessment of "the ability to use skills and knowledge with the functional competence needed for meeting the requirements of adult living."[22] This is the reasoning behind a 1975 study conducted by the University of Texas which attempted to measure the performance level of adults in carrying out a number of tasks.

The study examined the "competency" of a sample of 7,500 adults in areas of knowledge and skill deemed necessary for adult living. Those areas included occupational knowledge, consumer economics, government and law, health, community resources, reading, problem solving, computation, and writing. The study interviewed respondents and determined their levels of competency in each of these areas. Aggregating the results into an overall competency index, the APL study associated levels of competency with measures of performance such as income, job status, and education. Looking at the relationship between competency and adult performance, the APL study identified three levels of competency:

APL 1: those adults whose mastery of competency objectives is associated with inadequate income of poverty level or less, eight years of school or less, unemployment, or low job status.

APL 2: those adults whose mastery of competency objectives is associated with income of more than the poverty level but no discretionary income, education of nine to eleven years of school and occupations falling in the middle of the job status range.

APL 3: those adults whose mastery of competency objectives is associated with high levels of income, high levels of education including high school completion or more, and high levels of job status.

In effect, the APL study determined levels of competency in relation to the characteristics of the groups with various performances in life. This approach was aimed at associating the competencies of reading and writing, for example, with the performance of earning a high income. As a result, the APL approach measured both the levels of functioning of the sample and their performance in society, at least as measured by income, level of education completed, job status, and other indicators.

The results of the APL study indicated that large numbers of Americans, judged by the combination of their competencies and performance, had difficulty in functioning. As mentioned earlier in this chapter, about 20 percent of the adult population were functioning at APL level 1, defined as "adults who function with difficulty." An additional 34 percent of adults functioned at APL level 2, "functional adults." Only 46 percent of adults functioned at the third competency level, "proficient adults."

The APL study defined the outer limits in the debate about the extent of illiteracy, while associating the results with actual performance in adult life. The relationships of these results to definitions of "literacy" and "illiteracy" are very subjective. The problem with this approach is that it is circular. Functional skills are associated with economic and educational levels of people and then those levels are used to define literacy.

If one assumes that adults who have competencies that lead them to situations involving the characteristics that resemble APL 1 are "illiterate", then about 20 percent of the adult population is "illiterate" or "functionally illiterate." If one assumes that adults in the category of APL 2 are "functionally illiterate", then about 49 million people in the United States are "functionally illiterate." The APL approach to estimating the size of the population in need of literacy enhancement is based on a definition of economic performance. By this measure the size of the problem is between 23 and 49 million people, or roughly 20 to 54 percent of the adult population.

School Completion As a Proxy for Literacy

Although policymakers recognize that school completion may not reflect true literacy, the strong correlation between years of school completed and other measures of literacy or adult functioning suggest that the old method of estimating literacy rates based on information about schooling may not be far off. Despite many anecdotal, and probably factual, stories about "illiterates" graduating from American high schools, measurements of literacy based on school completion reveal much about the general level of literacy among the adult population.

In using school completion information to estimate literacy rates, the basic question remains a definitional one: what level of educational completion defines "literacy?" Various definitions include the following: at least six years of school (Census), the completion of at least the eighth grade (a military definition), and high school graduation (another common assertion).

Based on Census estimates, the facts are:

- In 1980 about 2.4 percent of the population over age 25 had failed to complete five years of school,
- In 1980 about 4 percent had eight years of schooling or less,
- In 1986 the national rate of high school graduation was 70.6 percent,

31

• The average years of schooling nationally was 12.6 according to the 1980 Census.

If one is willing to use 1980 data, the Census provides detailed, state-by-state information on school completion: adults over the age of twenty who had completed four years or less of school, eight years or less of school, or one to three years of high school; as well as those who had graduated from high school or beyond. Larger percentages of adults failed to complete the eighth grade in the South. States with large numbers of recent immigrants and rural states exhibit low school completion rates. Dropout rates are high in states with large central cities and with substantial immigration as well as in the South. Dropout rates or high school graduation rates can be used to estimate the number of young adults who did not receive high school diplomas in recent years. For higher levels of literacy, a comparison of post-secondary attendance data and high school graduation data will indicate how many adults have graduated from high school but not pursued further education.

THE SHAPE OF THE LITERACY CONTINUUM

Based on these four ways of estimating the incidence of literacy and illiteracy in America, we can draw some inferences about the shape of the literacy continuum. These inferences can help policymakers understand how their state fits into the national literacy situation.

(1) If the the governor's primary interest is adults with the lowest level of literacy skills and who are relatively young potential workers, the number across the nation is probably less than 5 percent, although it may be larger in states with high numbers of minorities, large central cities, and large numbers of recent immigrants. This group of adults is unable to accomplish the simplest of decoding tasks

in reading or computation, and, as a result, is likely to be unemployed or employable only at the lowest-skill jobs available.

(2) A somewhat larger group of adults — perhaps an additional 10 percent of the adult population — has great difficulty in reading, writing, and computing, although they manage to work, support families, raise children, and survive. This group is composed primarily of white Americans, although blacks and Hispanics are disproportionately represented. As many as a third to a half of the minority adult population falls into this group. Older workers, some of whom face displacement as the economy changes, are also disproportionately represented in this group.

(3) A much larger group of adults has attained basic levels of proficiency in coding and decoding but has difficulty in information processing, solving problems and the application of basic reading and computation skills to complex situations. This group could amount to half the adult population of the United States.

(4) Among recent immigrants, the urban poor, and in remote rural areas, the percentages of adults in groups (1) and (2) are very high, perhaps over half. Among welfare recipients and prisoners, the fractions falling into categories (1) and (2) may approach two-thirds to three-fourths. Some estimates are that over 80 percent of inmates of correctional institutions are "functionally illiterate."

No state situation will conform to the national estimates, no matter which set of definitions and methodologies are adopted. Each state staff will have to make its own estimates based on the needs of the political decision makers. To do so, state policy and planning officials will have to focus attention on the most important parts of the literacy continuum and utilize as much information as possible from within their own states. To guide the process of making estimates for the governor, the following questions may be helpful:

What is the overall policy goal that the governor is attempting to achieve in setting out to develop a strategy of enhance adult literacy?

The governor's goal may be to improve job prospects or to help support education reforms. The governor may want to focus attention on older workers or upon recent high school graduates in order to support an economic development strategy. Based on the goals of the governor, the policy and planning staff can narrow the definitional task.

At what point or range within the literacy continuum should attention be focused?

The answer to this question will reflect the policy priorities of the governor or other decision makers in a state attempting to secure useful estimates. If the primary purpose for pursuing the issue of literacy is to improve job prospects and increase the productivity of the state's economy, the governor will be best served by defining literacy in the context of what the private sector believes are adequate job skills. This point will not be the same for all states, but will vary according to the type of economic development occurring. It may be, for example, that the appropriate target on the literacy continuum will be higher in Michigan, where strategists are pursuing complex manufacturing as an economic base, than in Florida, where much of the projected job growth is expected to be in relatively low-skill service occupations.

Broadly speaking, what populations are the most important to assess?

If the primary goal of the governor is to reduce welfare and other economic dependency, then state policy planners know that estimating literacy levels among single-parents will be more important than estimating literacy levels among the elderly. Similarly, if the governor's goal is to overcome the effects of years of racial discrimination or to help recent immigrants assimilate into the state's economy, estimating the literacy levels of racial and ethnic minority groups will be more important than learning about the literacy levels of all young adults.

What characteristics do policymakers need to know about those populations?

For both measurement purposes and to help design policy strategies, how much must we know about those on the literacy continuum? Once again, assessing the governor's overarching policy goals will help narrow the search. If literacy of current workers is the primary concern of the governor, we need to know where current workers fall on the literacy scale and how many of them are likely to be displaced because of changes in the economic environment. We are not as concerned initially about their families, their ethnicity or their communities as we are about their jobs and workplaces. If, on the other hand, the governor's goals relate primarily to reducing welfare dependency, we will need to search for more information about the characteristics of welfare families, only one of which is the place on the literacy continuum of the head of the household.

What state-specific indicators are available to get a "real world" or common sense grasp of the extent of the literacy problem?

Large amounts of information are generated by state programs and through state operations that are not directly aimed at measuring literacy but which can be used to cross-check other estimating procedures. A few of these sources of additional information include:

- How many people request the oral drivers' license examination? What is the percentage of these adults compared to the total number taking the exam?[23]
- How does the state's adult education plan define and measure literacy?
- What is the experience of young adults in taking the armed forces entrance examinations?
- What do interviews with employers indicate about the preparedness of entry-level and other employees for jobs? What is the experience of state agencies who recruit new employees, especially agencies that offer entry-level jobs?
- What do providers of adult education report concerning the skill levels of those entering adult education programs. Similarly, what do providers of adult vocational education report about the average skill levels of people seeking vocational and technical education?
- What are the literacy levels encountered by vocational rehabilitation counselors as they work to rehabilitate injured or disabled workers?
- How do prisoners perform on tests when they seek education in correctional institutions?
- How do potential enrollees in JTPA (Job Training Partnership Act) programs perform on tests for basic skills? Do large numbers of them require basic education and remediation before moving on to skills training?
- Are large percentages of young people in high school enrolled in special education programs?
- What do welfare and social services agencies report about the literacy of their clients? Do clients have great difficulty in filling out forms such as monthly reporting forms for welfare and food stamps?

- Does the revenue department report problems in filling out tax forms and on other reporting requirements?

Gathering information from employers, state program operations, and other sources will help to create a more detailed picture of the literacy continuum in the state.

What is the purpose of securing these estimates? How will the estimates be used?

To what degree is "microanalysis" of the literacy of a population necessary, or can rougher judgments inform the policy process just as well? In describing the population of a state in terms of their literacy skills, it may be that substantial subgroups do not have to be described in detail, since there is little likelihood of their becoming the focus of gubernatorial or legislative attention. Literacy skills among immigrants over age sixty-five, for example, tend to be less than among the population as a whole, but unless the governor's goals include a strong emphasis on literacy for older workers, policy and planning officials will not have to know much about the skill levels of the elderly in order to meet the governor's needs. If the governor's goals in the short term are simply to raise public awareness of the literacy problem, relatively sweeping generalizations about the literacy of the entire population will suffice. If he or she is seriously exploring policy options to present to the legislature and the public during the next budget cycle, however, much more detailed analysis will be necessary.

METHODOLOGIES FOR STATE-SPECIFIC ESTIMATES

In developing estimates for describing the continuum of literacy in any state, two broad approaches appear to be useful. The first involves setting thresholds and estimating the number of people who fall below them, but not where they fall. The second determines skill levels of some populations and generalizes to fill in gaps in knowledge about actual literacy levels. In most cases, state officials will want to use a combination of approaches to sketch the shape of the literacy continuum.

Setting and Measuring Thresholds of Literacy

One approach to estimating literacy levels is to choose a definition of literacy, such as years of school completed, then lump all those who fall below that level as "illiterate" or "functionally illiterate." Despite the evidence and exhortation of scholars of adult literacy that literacy skills lie on a continuum and that one person's literacy is another's illiteracy, many political leaders and advocates prefer to make arbitrary definitional distinctions and count the "literate" and the "illiterate." In fact, a recent summary of activities of statewide literacy coalitions — most of which were appointed by the governor — indicates that this approach is the predominant one in the real world of political decision-making and policy development.

Officials in many states have defined "illiteracy" according to definitions reviewed earlier in this guide. They have felt it necessary to create arbitrary thresholds or cut-off points on the literacy continuum in order to proceed with the public awareness campaigns or policy development for the governor or legislature. Most officials are uncomfortable with this approach, but like other facts of life in state government, they live with it. In some states, this approach is justified by the fact that even arbitrary distinctions between the "illiterate" and the "literate" generate such large numbers of adults who need assistance that current service programs only serve a small percentage. Methodological purity gives way to practicality. While we would all like to be more accurate, they reason, there are so few resources to serve the "illiterate" that we need to move on to program development without arguing about definitions or estimates.

Attempting to Describe the Literacy Continuum with Available Data

A more ambitious and comprehensive approach would be to describe the population of a state in terms of its distribution along the literacy skills continuum and then to focus attention on the characteristics of people in certain "band widths" of that continuum.

To do so, it is necessary to take a "building block" approach: estimate the percentages of adults at various levels of the literacy skill continuum and add them up. Using the various national studies of adult functioning and literacy skills, policy planners can make some bold assumptions about their applicability to particular states, stretching their findings to help generate rough estimates.

For example:

(1) Take the ELPS 1982 results and apply them to more recent demographic and social characteristic data in the state.

(2) Associate the ELPS cut-off with a NAEP score, probably about 200 on the NAEP literacy scale.

(3) Apply the NAEP results to a broader range of adults, possible those adults who are between the ages of eighteen and thirty-five or twenty-one and forty-five. Since the NAEP reported that there was an increase in literacy skills among adults age twenty-one to twenty-five compared to seniors in high school, applying those results to those older than twenty-one might be more appropriate. The logic

behind extending the NAEP results is an imperfect one: assuming that the educational system changes only very slowly, there is reason to believe that skills imparted to those age twenty-one to twenty-five are probably much the same as skills imparted to people over twenty-five, at least up to the ages of thirty-five or forty. In a state with large numbers of immigrants who have not experienced the public school system, this assumption may not hold, but for most states this assumption seems reasonable.

(4) Using the social and demographic characteristic breakdowns reported in the NAEP study, adjust the NAEP results for the characteristics of adults in the state. In particular, the NAEP reported that literacy skills fell off more rapidly among minority citizens and those with less schooling than among others. Applying these percentages to the percentages of people with these character-istics in the state will generate better estimates than applying the averages reported for the national sample.

(5) For those over age thirty-five or forty-five, utilize school completion statistics to complete the rough description of the literacy continuum. In using school completion or years of schooling data, however, one must be careful not to double count those who might fall under the ELPS cut-off. As a result, estimators will have to equate a school completion year with the ELPS cut-off, another difficult but necessary assumption.

(6) Take a look at the APL 1 and APL 2 data to see if the literacy continuum described in steps (1) through (5) roughly corre-sponds with the levels of functioning predicted by the APL in the state.

(7) Enrich the information derived through the applica-tion of the methods in steps (1) through (5) with state-specific information from state government operations, providers of literacy services, and the private sector. Since the governor's goals will relate to literacy in the work force, a strong emphasis on tying occupational literacy requirements will generate the best information for the governor.

By defining the literacy continuum and estimating the numbers and characteristics of people along that continuum, state policy and planning officials will be able to give governors the clearest picture of the adult literacy problem without pre-judging how many people are "illiterate" or "literate". With information on the extent of the problem, the governor and state staff can make key decisions about what part of the continuum and which population groups need assistance in improving literacy skills. In the longer term, state officials may want to design and implement studies using the NAEP approach for the entire adult population or sub-groups, such as potentially displaced workers. In this manner, states could develop literacy profiles that would inform policymaking for years to come. Since it is unlikely that state actions can solve the problems of adult illiteracy in the short term, investing state resources to determine the baseline of literacy in a state will pay large benefits in the quality of policy and program design.

Chapter 2 Notes

1. David Harman, *Illiteracy: A National Dilemma* (New York: Cambridge Book Company, 1987), 3.
2. Ibid.,2.
3. UNESCO established this defnition in 1951. See Employment and Training Administration, "Illiteracy in America: Background Notes" (Washington, D.C., July, 1986, unpublished), 3.
4. Robert H. Cahen, "Illiteracy As An Economic Development Issue," (Youngstown, Ohio: The Center for Urban Studies, Youngstown State University, June, 1986), 4.
5. U.S. Department of Commerce, Bureau of the Census, *State and Metropolitan Area Data Book,* 1986 (Washington, D.C.: U.S. Government Printing Office, April, 1986).
6. Irwin S. Kirsch and Ann Jungeblut, *Literacy: Profiles of America's Young Adults*

(Princeton: Educational Testing Service, 1987), 3.

7. U.S. Department of Education, "Adult Literacy Estimates for States" (Washington, D.C.: Office of Planning, Budget and Evaluation, 1986, unpublished).

8. Carman St. John Hunter and David Harman, *Adult Illiteracy in the United States: A Report to the Ford Foundation* (New York: McGraw Hill, 1985), 7.

9. David Harman, *Illiteracy: A National Dilemma* (New York: Cambridge Book Company, 1987), 7.

10. Adult Performance Level Project, The University of Texas at Austin, Office of Continuing Education, *Adult Functional Competency: A Summary* (Austin, Texas: The Adult Performance Level Project, 1975).

11. Employment and Training Administration, "Illiteracy in America: Background Notes" (Washington, D.C., July, 1986, unpublished), 3.

12. See R. Timothy Rush, Alden J. Moe and Rebecca L. Storlie, *Occupational Literacy Education* (Newark, Delaware: International Reading Association, 1986).

13. Richard Venezky, et. al., *The Subtle Danger* (Princeton, New Jersey: Educational Testing Service, 1987), 3.

14. U.S. Department of Education, "Adult Literacy Estimates for States" (Washington, D.C.: Office of Planning, Budget and Evaluation, 1986, unpublished), 2.

15. Irwin S. Kirsch and Ann Jungeblut, *Literacy: Profiles of America's Young Adults* (Princeton: Educational Testing Service, 1987), 3.

16. Ibid.,v.

17. Ibid., 19.

18. Ibid., 5.

19. Ibid., 64.

20. Richard Venezky, et. al., *The Subtle Danger* (Princeton, New Jersey: Educational Testing Service, 1987), 30-41.

21. Irwin S. Kirsch and Ann Jungeblut, *Literacy: Profiles of America's Young Adults* (Princeton: Educational Testing Service, 1987), 5.

22. Adult Performance Level Project, The University of Texas at Austin, Office of Continuing Education, *Adult Functional Competency: A Summary* (Austin, Texas: The Adult Performance Level Project, 1975), 1.

23. See, for example, Patricia F. Waller and Robert G. Hall, "Classified Licensing: Development of Procedrues and Materials, Volume IV" (Chapel Hill, North Carolina: University of North Carolona, Highway Safety Research Center, 1976).

CHAPTER 3

ADULT LITERACY AND GUBERNATORIAL POLICY: A TARGETED APPROACH

INTRODUCTION

In Chapter Two, we discussed how the process of defining literacy and measuring where adults fit on the literacy continuum should be informed by the policy goals of the governor. At the same time, the governor needs to consider how the current literacy of the population affects other state policy goals, particularly those related to improving economic development, reducing dependency, and enhancing educational opportunities. From a state policy perspective, the governor must make basic decisions not only about the policies and programs needed to enhance literacy generally, but also about priorities in terms of targeting resources. In addition, the governor must make some important judgments about what state government can do about the problem and about the role of the private sector and other major institutions in the state.

This chapter addresses the key steps that staff members must take as they help political decision makers develop policies and programs to enhance adult literacy. These steps include:

- Relating policy analysis to policy goals;
- Targeting the analysis of the problem; and,
- Defining the state role in addressing the issue.

Given the extent and complexity of the problems of adult literacy and the limited resources to deal with them, only a disciplined analysis and decision-making process will enable state officials to develop policies and programs that will show results.

RELATING LITERACY POLICY TO OTHER POLICY GOALS

In a different world, political executives might pursue the goal of adult literacy as an end unto itself. Since the citizens of our state and nation basically value education as enriching life, governors might strive to improve the reading, writing, and reasoning abilities of the population as part of a strategy to enrich the cultural life of the state or simply to help people live better. In the current economic and political environment, however, the governor's attention to adult literacy is very likely to be grounded in its relationship to other goals such as providing good jobs, improving education, or stimulating the creation of new firms.

In developing a useful analysis of the literacy issue for the governor, state policy and planning officials need to focus clearly on the broader policy goals that an adult literacy initiative is expected to address. Both advocates for adult literacy and policy analysts must understand the policy context in which the search for solutions to the "literacy problem" is likely to be addressed by political decision-makers. In short, policy planners must have at least a rough understanding of the motivations of their bosses in addressing the issue before the work of policy analysis can begin.

At the same time, the nature of the problem of adult literacy means that many misconceptions must be uprooted before the definitional work, the measurement of the problem, and the development of state strategies can begin. As we have seen in Chapter Two, defining literacy is not easy; the best definitions involve a continuum of skills that are difficult to measure. Most citizens and most officials probably believe otherwise: that people are "illiterate" or "literate" and that if we could just somehow make the "illiterate" literate, many of our economic and social problems would be solved.

Since the motivations of political officials in addressing adult literacy are very likely to be tied to how "erasing illiteracy" can help solve other problems, these misconceptions about literacy can color the way in which a governor or legislature approaches the issue. The job of the policy planner is to understand the larger policy goals of state officials and to dispel some of the misconceptions about literacy and the role of policies to enhance literacy in achieving other goals. Some hypothetical examples may serve to clarify this relationship.

State A: A Clash Between Policy Goals and Literacy Realities

Because the governor has been a businessperson, a state legislator for twelve years, and grew up in our state, he knows that adult literacy is a serious problem. He knows, for example, that our state's large population of recent immigrants, together with a history of low investment in education, means that we have large numbers of adults whose position on the literacy scale is very low.

At the same time, our governor has articulated an economic development strategy that demands very highly skilled people and an education reform strategy that focuses on "excellence." Programs have recently been enacted that fund reduced class sizes and special programs for the gifted and mandate stricter graduation standards. Teachers will be paid more, a career ladder program is expected to help retain the best teachers, and a large bond issue will provide new facilities for the public schools.

The governor is aware, however, that 80 percent of the labor force for the next twenty years is already out of school. No amount of reform in elementary and secondary schools will affect the economic development prospects in the state in the near future, except that the atmosphere of reform may encourage current businesses to stay in the state and expand.

The governor is receiving mixed messages from the business community. One group of businesspeople — those with firms in the service sector — is telling him that they have trouble getting workers with even the most basic skills. A smaller but growing group of businesspeople who are providing new jobs in complex manufacturing, research, and technology, says that their problem lies in finding employees who can be trained to do more difficult tasks and can reason their way through problems on the job site.

In the last negotiation with legislative leaders and teacher representatives over raising teacher salaries, the teachers warned the governor that his education reforms might be endangered by the abysmally low level of preschool preparedness, especially in remote rural areas and the two big cities in the state. The Education Department blamed part of that problem on too little day care, but most of it was blamed on the inability of parents to read to their children.

The governor has asked that we give him an analysis of the adult literacy situation in the state. He doesn't want policy options yet, just some estimates of the problem and suggestions for how an adult literacy strategy might fit into his other priorities. He wants to decide whether or not to focus further analysis and political attention on the issue, or whether to concentrate on other pressing issues, such as prison overcrowding.

In approaching this issue, we first attempt to clarify what policy goals the governor is pursuing that will be enhanced by attention to the problem of adult literacy. In this case, there seem to be three goals related to economic development and education:

(1) To upgrade basic skills in the labor force to fight unemployment and welfare dependency and, he hopes, to reduce crime;

(2) To support high wage, high value-added industry, particularly technology-related firms that are growing rapidly; and,

(3) To support education improvement for the long term through improvements in early childhood education.

Our second problem is developing estimates of the literacy problem, based on our understanding of the governor's policy goals and motivations for addressing the issue. At the same time, we want to do so in a way that will stress that literacy is a continuum of skills, not an absolute.

As a result of the examination of the continuum of literacy described in Chapter Two, we have developed a rough idea of the shape of literacy in our state. While we have not neglected the entire continuum, we have tried to look closely at two "bands" of skills on the literacy continuum. In the first "band," we lump skills employers believe are absolutely essential for most minimum wage jobs and skills that educators say are minimal for parental involvement in preschool education. The second "band" of skills on the continuum are those demanded by the growing research and technology sector of our economy. These involve not only reading, writing, and computing but working through problems with groups and communicating results.

We struggle to get employers, educators, and literacy experts to relate these skill levels to indicators that will let us measure the rough numbers for presentation to the governor. No one will commit him or herself, but through repeated efforts we gain enough knowledge to make some assumptions:

(1) We decide that in the first "band" we will include those adults who would either not pass the ELPS (considered by state staff to be a very basic level of literacy) or who might pass it but would fall

below the 250 level of the NAEP (were that test given to all adults rather than just those age twenty-one to twenty-five.) We will cross-check any estimates derived from using these methods with data on school completion and an application of variables in the lowest part of the APL.

Through application of the NAEP and the ELPS method-ologies we "guestimate" that the portion of our adult population who would score below 250 on the NAEP or fall only slightly above the cutoff on the ELPS test may exceed 20 percent. This estimate seems to track with the number of adults in the population who have not achieved 9th grade.

This represents almost 1.8 million people, about two-thirds as large as the number of children currently attending public elementary and secondary schools. Over half of this group are Black or Hispanic and about a quarter are recent immigrants. Compared to the rest of the population they are young and most are employed, despite our definition that they have few skills for employment. The group encompasses 80 percent of our welfare recipients and 90 percent of our prisoners but is much larger than both populations together. This is a very large and daunting number to present to the governor.

(2) We decide that in the second "band" of skills, we will consider adults who have completed high school but have no post-secondary education. On the NAEP scale, this group would fall between about 300 and 350, we believe, or would be in the upper level of the APL 2 group. Looking at high school graduation statistics, post-secondary enrollments and the NAEP national estimates, we "guestimate" that about 2.8 million adults fall into this category: another very large number for the governor to consider.

Most of the people in this group are white. Many live in small towns and rural areas or on the urban fringe of the two large cities. Since our state has no history of large, blue collar industry, we assume that many of these people are currently employed in light manufacturing, retail trade and distribution occupations, and support services for farming, ranching, and extractive industries.

In making our estimates, we have taken into consideration what we believe to be the primary policy interests of the governor and we have narrowed our focus to concentrate on estimating the problem in terms of policy goals. We would not bet our jobs on the accuracy of our estimates. We have learned several things, however:

(1) In approaching the problem of literacy from the perspective of the governor's goals of upgrading basic skills for economic development, supporting education reform, and helping high value-added industries, we are dealing with very large numbers of people.

(2) A cursory review of the adult education priorities and job training system in our state reveals that there is little match between the services provided, such as the GED program, and the priorities inherent in applying the governor's goals to the estimating problem.

(3) Very few of the adults identified in our estimates voted for the governor in the last election. His was a suburban, downtown business, rancher and farmer coalition.

The governor and his key advisers can receive an initial briefing. In the briefing, we will concisely present the following points and ask for further guidance:

- Literacy is a continuum of skills and definitions are difficult.
- Based on our best assessment of policy goals and literacy measures, two key groups of adults in our state are the most likely targets for developing strategies to enhance literacy. These groups are those with minimal skills (about 1.8 million) and those with skills that could

be enhanced to help fuel the growth of high value-added businesses (about 2.8 million).

- Together, these groups amount to more people than there are now children in our elementary and secondary education system, and four times the enrollment of our post-secondary institutions.

- To take the next step in developing a meaningful adult literacy strategy, we need to set narrower parameters, to target populations likely to be more critical to achieving the governor's goals.

- We recommend that the governor focus his attention and political capital on sub-groups of each larger group. These include:
  — Welfare recipients and prisoners with minimal skills;
  — Non-English speaking recent immigrants;
  — Recent high school graduates on the urban fringe who have not sought post-secondary education; and,
  — Returning military personnel with high school equivalency skills.

The basis of these suggestions is partly related to our ability to serve people with limited resources, partly related to cost avoidance in welfare and corrections, and partly related to the special need to assimilate immigrants into the economy on the heels of the new immigration law. In addition, focusing on these subgroups enables us to serve people not now served by existing education or welfare systems. The selection of these subgroups reinforces the governor's overall economic development and education priorities.

State B: Literacy in a Mature Economy

State B's situation has some similarities to State A, but there are critical differences that will lead the governor to different conclusions about how to approach the problem of adult literacy.

Reelected after four years of dealing with a rapidly deteriorating and then reviving economy, the governor has decided to do whatever she can to restructure the economy in our state so that this type of depression can never happen again. She commissions an economic development study that concludes that our state should build on its strength in manufacturing technology. No longer, says the study, can we rely on mechanical power and relatively unskilled labor to compete in manufacturing. We must integrate information processing with high technology manufacturing processes in order to survive. In addition, many new jobs will be created as a result of our strong university system and technological spin-offs. New technologies in agriculture and forestry need to be encouraged in order to stabilize those sectors of our economy.

The governor knows that, despite a relatively heavy investment in education over the years, the literacy of some parts of our population is still rudimentary at best. Especially troubling are large minority populations in our two large, old central cities. Equally important to the governor, however, are large numbers of young people who have grown up in smaller mill towns or blue collar sections of our older cities. These young people, she believes must get more education and upgrade literacy skills if they are to be capable of operating a newer, more complex manufacturing economy. Yet she believes that the history of their families and communities has led them to take education less seriously, because "if I drop out, I can always get work in the factory." In the governor's view, convincing these young adults that they must enhance their literacy skills in order to compete in a more demanding economy is the primary challenge in addressing the adult literacy issue.

51

The governor has exhibited a strong commitment to education, but the fiscal situation in the state in recent years has made "holding our own" a major accomplishment. Until recently, there have been no extra funds for expansion of preschool programs, little money to raise teachers salaries, and the universities have been squeezed hard. As the economy turned up, the governor chose to put new resources primarily into the university system on a selective basis, driven by the "technology spin-off" argument. Lately, there has been serious talk in the governor's office about "welfare reform" but this package has not yet been formulated.

The governor has asked that we assess the adult literacy situation in the state and recommend an approach for next year's budget and State of the State cycle.

In State B, the governor has already spent five years articulating and clarifying her policy priorities: she wants to aid restructuring the economy and she is willing to consider bold action to accomplish that goal. All other goals are secondary to the economic development priority. In addition, while she is concerned with the literacy of the very poor and the quality of the schools in the inner city, her primary economic policy focus is on the sons and daughters of blue collar workers who are being challenged to make the economic transition she sees so clearly.

Examining the available literacy measurement tools, the policy and planning office observes that the ELPS approach seems much too rudimentary to measure the skill levels of the group important to the governor. The NAEP seems ideally suited to the task. Although the NAEP assessment is confined to adults age twenty-one to twenty-five, we feel confident that its basic conclusions apply to a broader age group, perhaps eighteen- to thirty-year-olds. We examine more closely the social and economic characteristics of those in the NAEP sample who scored between 250 and 350 on most scales. We work back from the characteristics of the NAEP sample, roughly adjusting the NAEP findings to the socioeconomic characteristics of the young adults in our state. We have more minority young adults than the sample but our school completion rate is higher than the national average. Adjusting for these factors and applying the NAEP percentages to our population of adults from the ages of eighteen to thirty, we estimate that there are about two million young adults that fall into the category that the governor has implicitly identified.

At the same time, we note that our high school graduation rate is about 78 percent, meaning that about 22 percent of State B's ninth graders do not receive their high school diplomas. About 28 percent of all State B's adults have not graduated from high school, but only about 6 percent of those failed to finish the ninth grade. Because high school graduation rates have increased over the years, we estimate that about 18 percent of young adults from the ages of eighteen to thirty have not graduated from high school but have finished the ninth grade. This estimate tracks with the broader NAEP estimate based on skill levels. We "guestimate" for the governor, then, that the target group we are examining has about 360,000 adults. Most of them are white but about 40 percent are from minority groups.

Considering the post-secondary enrollment in our state, this is a large but not unmanageable number. We recommend to the governor that we focus the analysis of adult literacy on adults who have completed the ninth grade but have not completed high school. For students currently in school, the governor has asked that a dropout prevention program be developed in addition to the investigation of adult literacy policy alternatives. In the adult literacy analysis, we will focus on adults age twenty-one to twenty-five who have finished the ninth grade but have not graduated from college. We will pay especially close attention to those who are currently employed but who are at great risk of becoming displaced workers.

State C: Overcoming Educational Deficits

The governor of State C has waged a two-year battle with the legislature to approve what for his state is a far-reaching education reform package, but he recognizes that much more needs to be done. The state's economy is based on farming, low-wage manufacturing, and tourism. Still struggling to catch up with the rest of the nation after decades of racial conflict and underinvestment, the state's fiscal and political structure can barely sustain the changes that he has sought to make in his first three years in office.

The governor knows first hand of the poverty and educational deficits borne by both blacks and whites in State C. Although he has accomplished much in education reform by associating in the public mind better education with jobs and economic development, he also knows that improving elementary and secondary education is only a long-term solution to the economic woes that chronically beset the state. Last week, when speaking on education reform to a group of high school seniors, he asked all those who planned to stay in State C to raise their hands. Only a sprinkling of hands were visible in the rural high school auditorium.

The Department of Education reports that the two greatest challenges faced by the schools in implementing the education reforms mandated by the governor and legislature are dealing with inadequate preschool preparation and preventing students from dropping out. State C has only a few, federally funded, Headstart preschool programs and suffers the highest dropout rate in the nation. Businesspeople tell the governor that most high school dropouts have so few skills that they are suited only for low skill work on farms and in manufacturing assembly operations. Despite efforts to attract industry, the state's economic development agency reports that the number of low skilled jobs is actually shrinking.

The governor has asked the policy and planning office to assess the literacy problem and provide advice concerning the best places to start in confronting what he knows is a massive problem.

A quick look at the numbers confirms the governor's impression. The ELPS study indicates that about 16 percent of State C adults function at a very basic level in terms of English language proficiency. The APL numbers are even more disturbing. Applying APL 1 characteristics to data on the state population, about 40 percent of the adults in the state are likely to be "functionally illiterate." Although the NAEP nationwide results indicate that many of those who are function at the lower end of the literacy scale are older victims of years of underinvestment in schooling, the characteristics of the State C young adult population indicates that a greater percentage of young adults here function at a 250 level or lower than in the rest of the nation. For adults with young children, the percentages are likely to be even higher, since fertility rates among minority groups in the state are higher than among whites. Over 700,000 adults in this small, rural state are likely to be at the low end of the literacy continuum. By contrast, the elementary and secondary school enrollment is only about 465,000.

Of the 700,000 adults functioning at this very low literacy level, about 125,000 have preschool children. At present, literacy enhancement programs reach only about 12,000 adults with preschool children through JTPA (Job Training Partnership Act) supported job training and job readiness programs, adult vocational education programs and in the adult basic education programs delivered by local community colleges.

The policy staff also notes that about 18,000 adult welfare recipients with small children have very low literacy levels. The policy and planning staff recommend to the governor a targeted approach to literacy designed to help parents with small children. They recommend a goal of literacy enhancement for all 18,000 welfare recipients and another 30,000 adults with small children over a four-year period.

The governor is uncomfortable that little is proposed for workers who may want to upgrade their literacy skills but decides that with limited resources available, the best strategy for targeting the analysis is to focus on adults with young children so that the education reform he is pursuing will be strengthened by efforts to improve literacy. He instructs staff to ensure that any policy proposals brought to him during the budget process show how literacy training can be accompanied by efforts to involve parents in preschool preparation.

TARGETING THE ANALYSIS

As the hypothetical examples related in the previous section illustrate, one of the major functions of the policy planner in dealing with the subject of adult literacy will be to target the analysis to a manageable level. There are several reasons that a targeted approach will be necessary:

(1) In most states, the population who would benefit from literacy enhancement in order to pursue broad gubernatorial goals will be very large. Using a shotgun approach to policy analysis will likely cause political decision makers either to throw their hands up at the enormity of the problem or spread resources so thinly that little will be accomplished. Another reaction may be to consider the problem as being too vast and long-term for current political timeframes to accommodate. In the past, for example, some governors have looked at the adult literacy problem and decided that the best thing to do is to ignore it and hope that improvements in elementary and secondary schooling will solve the problem in the very long term.

(2) A broad-brush approach often leads only to symbolic action. Faced with a seemingly insurmountable problem, governors

and legislatures may legitimately feel that calling attention to the problem is the only rationale first step. Since decrying a problem is relatively inexpensive in the short run, a proliferation of commissions, studies, exhortations to others to act, and similar symbolic actions may well be the only result of a policy analysis that fails to target enough information to allow real action.

(3) Analysis that ascribes a problem to nearly everyone in the state, even if it is valid, is likely to be dismissed by politically pragmatic decision makers. In addition, focusing attention on the problem may contradict other important goals of the governor, such as promoting the success of earlier reforms or attracting industry. Announcing that "one-third of our workers are functionally illiterate" is not something that a governor is likely to do at the same time that he is touting the "skilled labor force" in his state in order to attract investment from Japan, for example.

(4) Without a targeted approach to the issue that enables a governor to set the agenda, special interests can easily "morselize" the problem. Every interest in the state government and many outside it will pick a small piece and claim that they are addressing adult literacy while actually doing little measurable to improve the situation. New bureaus or offices of adult literacy will spring up, mayors will announce "Adult Literacy Day" in their cities, school lobbies will call for more funds, and that will be that.

(5) Finally, and importantly, unless they target the analysis, state policymakers will not have enough information to judge whether the governor's policies have enhanced literacy levels, let alone whether literacy improvements have affected the larger policy problem being addressed by the governor. Intervention strategies cannot be designed precisely enough and measurement of results will be nearly impossible.

Targeting the analysis does not mean that policy planners should ignore the extent of the problem nor does it mean thinking small. In fact, casting the issue in a manageable form may be the only way to prevent the issue from dissipating in a wave of symbolism or being sliced up so thinly as to be ignored by the legislature or the bureaucracy.

Targeting the analysis involves several functions:

- *Presenting information that will allow the governor to decide what populations are most important to assist in enhancing literacy.* We must be able to draw a direct connection between the literacy of population groups and the overarching policy goals that motivate the governor in making difficult choices about where to focus his attention and the administration's fiscal or political resources. While it may seem self-evident, for example, that enhancing literacy of a welfare recipient will improve her chances of getting a good job, the governor is likely to ask whether this is merely a necessary condition or a sufficient condition for helping her achieve that goal. Without day care, health services and many other forms of assistance, helping her learn to read may not be directly connected to helping the governor reduce welfare costs or improve job prospects of the poor.

- *Developing detailed information on the characteristics of target populations.* The policy planner needs to present information on target populations that estimates not only current levels of literacy but also other characteristic relevant to designing policy strategies or program interventions. It is not enough to know that half the high school dropouts in a state function at a very low level of literacy. We must also know at least something about where they live, whether they are employed and,

if possible, in what sectors; if they have children in the
public schools; whether or not they are members of a
minority group; and, if possible, how many of them
interact with some government, corporate, or private
system that can help them enhance their literacy.

• *Showing that the governor's actions can actually affect
the target group.* Information about the targeted populations must be extensive enough so that there is reason
to believe that some government or private sector intervention can actually affect the problem. In short, the
governor must be convinced not only that people need
help but also that they can be reached and helped
successfully. This means that policy planners will have
to address issues of motivation, incentives, and community pressures, which will be discussed in a later portion
of this guide.

This function of the targeting analysis need not mean,
however, that we are limited to considering current programs, services, and strategies that now serve the potentially targeted population.
To limit ourselves at this point in the analysis would stifle creativity
and lead to incrementalism or "more of the same" when it comes time
to develop policies and strategies for dealing with literacy. It only
means that we think there is a reasonable possibility of affecting the
problem through concerted action.

By helping the governor select categories across the
continuum of literacy, we are not circumscribing his field of action
significantly. Indeed, at this point in the analysis we have hardly
begun to address policies, strategies and programs. This is not an
oversight, but an important point: *targeting should not be driven by
programs but by connecting gubernatorial goals to assessments of the
problem.*

If we are not careful, however, a targeting exercise designed to develop a manageable approach to a large problem can degenerate into a search for a quick and easy program-related answer. In state government, the process of narrowing the focus of policy development is often driven by a combination of haste and the dynamics of existing programs. A short example drawn loosely from recent experience in a governor's office will illustrate the problem.

As part of the process designed to generate policy options for the Governor's biennial budget and State of the State message, the issue of adult literacy was raised. Estimates of the problem were few and far between, but the policy and planning staff was able to say: "There are about 800,000 illiterate adults in our state, many of whom are likely to become displaced workers as our economy evolves." In addition, the governor was informed that the existing community college structure, which covered the state so that no person was more than fifty miles from a two-year institution, was judged to be relatively effective in providing adult education, especially through the GED program. "We now produce about 10,000 GEDs per year."

Presented with these two facts, the governor did the only thing he could be expected to do in the time he had: he authorized more funds for the community colleges and asked them to step up production of GEDs. GEDs were at least measurable, he reasoned. Aside from some other symbolic actions, such as calling a "Literacy Summit" in the state, the governor did little else. More substantive analysis and more comprehensive gubernatorial attention to the issue awaits the next biennium.

Despite the best of intentions, the mistake here was to let the existence of one delivery mechanism — the community colleges — drive the approach to the problem. The governor assumed:

- That many people were "illiterate," without understanding the continuum of literacy;

- That adult education leading to the GED addressed the problems of these people;
- That community colleges could enhance literacy of potentially displaced workers; and,
- That more money for the community colleges was the answer.

It is unlikely that all of these assumptions are true. More likely, the governor and the legislature have funded more GED training — possibly a worthy goal in its own right — expecting to "reduce illiteracy" and help "retrain potentially displaced workers." Neither goal is likely to be affected in any significant way.

In the hypothetical states A, B, and C, we can see how the policy and planning office narrowed the focus of the analysis, targeting the governor's attention on the parts of the literacy continuum that are most closely related to his other policy goals. In State A, for example, a two-staged approach was used. Based on the governor's priorities, policy planners first narrowed the examination of the literacy continuum to two broad groups: those with very limited literacy skills and those with skills well beyond the first group. Then a second round of analysis occurred, narrowing the target groups still further to a set of populations such as welfare recipients, recent immigrants, and high school graduates who had sought no post-secondary education. The criteria for narrowing the focus to these groups were not directly related to existing programs; in fact, the state had few programs that served these groups. The relationship of the targeting exercise was to the governor's goals and to other priorities, such as cost avoidance.

Similarly, in States B and C, the targeting process was driven by the governors' goals and perceptions of the economic problems faced by the state. In State B, the target was clear from the start: blue collar young adults who had not finished high school. Other concerns, such as welfare reform and prison overcrowding, were set aside because the pool of people in the target group was large and well defined, and because the lack of resources in the fiscally hard-hit State B dictated a well-focused approach.

In State C, the targets were more difficult to develop because of the magnitude of educational deficiencies throughout the state. Ultimately, the governor chose those with very limited literacy skills who had children. His approach was based on a long-term strategy of education reform rather than a shorter-term concern with the current labor force. He reasoned that enhancing parental literacy would benefit the economy directly in that their skills would increase, but that the major impact would be on the next generation of workers and citizens. Once again, the choice of this target group was not dictated by the availability of programs. In fact, State C had only recently strengthened its funding of elementary education and had done little to expand preschool programs that would help small children overcome parental literacy handicaps.

Obtaining agreement on targets for further analysis may be difficult. Special interest groups will resent the necessary process of exclusion that is implicit in targeting. Governors do not like to exclude explicitly some people from immediate assistance, although they do so implicitly every time they make a budget or policy decision. Nevertheless, in considering the policy issues surrounding adult literacy, targeting will be necessary, whether explicit as part of the policymaking process or implicit as programs are put in place.

THE IMPORTANCE OF DEFINING THE STATE ROLE

Even though the governor and his or her staff may have made some tentative decisions about what target groups on the literacy spectrum are most appropriate for further policy analysis, policy and planning staff should not jump to development of specific strategies or programs without careful analysis of the state role in enhancing literacy. Fundamental questions remain about the appropriate role of state government in motivating people to seek literacy enhancement, by providing services or inducing others to do so.

Some of these questions have only philosophical and value-laden answers; others are very practical. Once schooling is offered and completed or rejected, does the government have the responsibility to provide literacy or skills training? How far should state government go in helping the private sector obtain a skilled labor force? Are subsidies to motivate individuals or firms to obtain or provide literacy enhancing skills appropriate? Where are the lines between individual, private sector, and government responsibilities in providing literacy services?

Since enhancing literacy among adults requires a great deal of effort, how best can government intervene to help provide motivation, education and training and support services? What level of government is likely to have the best success at providing services? Can government do this at all, or is the role of state government to provide the regulatory and fiscal environment for community groups or private businesses to provide literacy enhancing services? All of these questions must be addressed in order to assess the appropriate approach to the problem from the governor's perspective. Once the role of state government is agreed upon, of course, the further question of the governor's role must be raised; but this issue will be addressed in a later part of this guide.

State government is a service provider, a regulator, and a fiscal agent. States provide direct services such as income maintenance, child welfare services, mental health services, and a variety of other institution-based services. They also directly regulate individuals by licensing motor vehicle use, hunting, fishing, barbers, beauticians, and a host of other activities performed by individuals. They regulate the provision of services by the private sector, such as banking and insurance.

For most services, however, the state is both a rule writer and a fiscal agent. In the public schools, states provide about half the money and write most of the regulations that govern elementary and secondary education. Higher education is overwhelmingly financed by state governments and many of the basic guidelines for the provision of post-secondary education are fashioned at the state level. Medical services for the poor are purchased as are a variety of other services, such as day care. Each of these purchasing programs comes with its own set of guidelines or regulations. States also set conditions for the receipt of benefits and services such as unemployment, welfare, social services, health care, and education.

In examining the state role, the limits of state government must also be considered. While large, state government is only a small part of the economy of any state. People's behaviors are seldom directly influenced by the activities of state government; most of the impact of state government is indirect. A school child's learning is clearly affected by state funding and rules, but this impact is mediated by local school boards, superintendents, principals, and teachers. The state government sets the rules for many forms of economic activity but it seldom has an immediate and direct influence on business formation, employment, incomes, or spending. The tools available to state government in addressing adult literacy, for example, are many; but most of them are indirect. Because the problem of adult literacy is a difficult and complex one, involving not only the provision of services but also the motivation of individuals to seek further education, state officials need to be aware of both the *reach* of state government and its *limits*.

State government can simply provide literacy services directly (although not necessarily efficiently) or it can require local governments, school districts, and others to provide those services. It can influence organizations, both public and private, to provide literacy enhancing services either through purchasing those services or granting funds to create literacy programs. The reach of state government is long.

On the other hand, state government has great difficulty intervening in individual behavior. It cannot stop the use of illicit drugs or alcohol, for example. It has a very hard time preventing teenage pregnancies. In spite of tremendous efforts, state governments have immense difficulty influencing the behavior of individuals in organizations such as schools, colleges, mental institutions, or even prisons. State government has an indirect effect on many behaviors but a direct effect on only a few.

Although the governor's policy and planning staff may have narrowed the focus of policy analysis to a well-defined group of individuals who need literacy enhancement, they should consider carefully the reach and limits of state government before they begin to examine policy alternatives for the governor. This means that the next step in the policy development process must be twofold:

- To assess the full range of powers and intervention tools available to state government for affecting the literacy of the target groups; and,
- To assess realistically the capability of state government to affect the desired outcome – moving a substantial number of people along the literacy spectrum in order to achieve a larger policy goal such as "jobs and productivity."

SUMMARY

In addressing the issue of enhancing adult literacy for jobs and productivity, this guide has recommended the following approach:

- Describe the literacy continuum with as much information as possible.
- Clarify the broad policy goals to which enhancing literacy is likely to be attached.
- Link the governor's policy goals with specific groups of people on the literacy continuum in order to narrow the focus of the analysis.
- Find out as much as you can about the characteristics of those groups; and,
- Consider the reach and limits of state government in affecting the literacy of those people before engaging in policy development or program design.

Engaging in this process will not be easy. The bureaucracy, adult literacy advocates, businesspeople, legislators, and others will approach the governor with their own targets and programs that promise to "solve" the problem. Current program providers will claim that more funding is necessary before new approaches can be taken. Political advisers to the governor may argue that setting targets unnecessarily excludes too many from the initiative. Others in state government, such as the superintendent of education, the chancellor of higher education or the president of the community college system, may feel that adult literacy is their primary responsibility, not the governor's. The governor may become impatient for program and policy ideas and not want to exercise the discipline necessary to link clearly economic development or education policies with adult literacy.

The governor and the policy staff must be firm and resolute in resisting pressures to jump to existing programs as solutions. Just as the definitions of adult literacy vary enormously and provide no one easy answer to the size and nature of the problem, the array of policy and program alternatives vary enormously and pose no easy solution. Prior to considering what should be done programmatically to upgrade literacy skills of the target populations, policymakers should carefully consider the full range of government powers and programs available that can be brought to bear on crafting a response.

STATE TOOLS FOR ENHANCING LITERACY

INTRODUCTION

Enhancing the literacy of adults will be a complex and difficult task. In order to ensure that policy strategies to promote literacy are effective, the governor will have to employ all the relevant tools and powers at his or her command and will need to influence many policies not under the governor's direct control. To be effective, state policies will need to be targeted correctly, implemented efficiently and evaluated frequently . The reasons that this undertaking will be more difficult than for many other state policies include the following:

- *Identifying those who will most benefit from enhanced literacy skills does not mean that they will want to seek them. The issue of motivation must be addressed.* Regardless of the target group or groups selected by the governor, people must be motivated to seek additional literacy skills. The process of enhancing literacy and gaining new skills is likely to be an arduous one. As Lewis Perelman has noted, the learning enterprise is the only industry in which the consumers do most of the work. [1] It seems likely that for many people, the long-term promise of better jobs or income will not be sufficient to motivate them to undertake or stick with the process of gaining additional literacy skills.

- *Compounding this motivational issue is the fact that traditional education systems have failed most of those who require additional skills.* Most of the people that adult literacy policies are trying to reach will have already been exposed to the traditional education system and will not have been successful. This lack of success deters them from seeking help in improving their skills. In addition, for many who have dropped out of school or otherwise failed to gain adequate skills, the classroom environment will not be conducive to learning. This means that the educational setting necessary for adult learning is likely to be quite different from the ones we are used to providing.

- *Even if target groups are well defined, there will be significant differences in skill levels, family and job circumstances, attitudes, and levels of commitment among those seeking to improve literacy.* If children in elementary and secondary schools require individualized instruction to excel, adults will require even more specialized approaches to learning. No one program or program type is likely to be sufficient to reach a single target group of people. Since most governors will identify multiple target populations, a mix of policies and programs will need to be developed in order for state policies to become effective.

- *State policies will have to address not only the learning of individuals but also the support of families and communities.* As David Harman observes, if literacy and higher level skills are not valued by the family and the community, any individual seeking to improve literacy will be fighting an uphill battle.[2] Just learning to read requires reinforcement. Acquiring the many other skills that a set of literacy enhancement policies and programs will attempt to inculcate will require much more support. Assistance to families and communities will be required in other areas as well. Among welfare recipients, for example, providing adult education will not be sufficient if child care, income, and health needs of families are not addressed.

- *The learning process takes a long time.* Whether the goal of policies is to move people on the literacy continuum from a very low level of skills to basic reading and writing (decoding) or to develop higher level learning skills, policies and programs will have to be in place for many years before significant results are accomplished. Since literacy itself is not the final goal of these policies, we can expect an additional time lag before better literacy is translated into better jobs, more productivity of the labor force, better prepared school children or even more informed voters.

For all these reasons, the search for strategies to enhance literacy will involve examining a very broad range of policy tools and program designs. The process of developing effective strategies and policies for the governor will cast a wide net, a net that encompasses state government as service provider as well as regulator, revenue collector, convener, coordinator and provider of resources.

In recent years, the job of combatting illiteracy or enhancing literacy in the public sector has been the province of the education system, with an occasional assist from the job training system. As governors become more ambitious about addressing adult literacy, the full range of state powers and responsibilities, functions, and roles should be assessed in order to develop strategies and policies that might successfully meet the challenge of enhancing literacy. In examining the array of powers and tools available to state government, we need to be aware of the basic functions we are trying to accomplish in developing policies to enhance literacy. These include:

- Identifying and reaching individuals with inadequate literacy skills;
- Motivating these individuals, recruiting them, and sustaining their interest;
- Delivering literacy services;
- Measuring individual progress along the continuum of literacy; and,
- Making the connection between enhanced literacy of individuals and other goals; such as better jobs, more income, less welfare, less crime or better school preparedness for their children.

Traditionally, programs have been funded and asked to accomplish all these functions as part of a single program design. This approach has been successful in only a few cases, because no single program design can accommodate all these difficult tasks. A broader approach is needed. What tools does state government have or can states develop to accomplish these functions?

In exploring the possible tools for enhancing literacy, we will examine the ways in which state government currently functions and the methods by which it influences individual behavior and private sector activity. This review is organized according to the generic functions of state government, rather than the traditional agency or issue-related breakdowns. This organizational structure may encourage policymakers to think about the application of all relevant powers and functions of states to the problem of adult literacy, not just the activities of the education, training, or human services agencies.

The functions of state government to be reviewed include:

- Direct service provision;
- Indirect service provision;
- Conditioning benefits and employment ;
- Using the tax system;
- Influencing private enterprise;
- Licensing individuals;
- Influencing local government responses; and,
- Providing leadership.

DIRECT SERVICE PROVISION

Depending upon the state, state government provides services directly to a large number of people, mostly in institutions (such as mental hospitals, institutions for the developmentally disabled, and prisons) and through state-operated social service and welfare programs. Many states operate public assistance programs and deliver child welfare services, although many others provide these services through counties or cities. State employment service offices provide job referrals and unemployment insurance. Semi-autonomous state universities and colleges also provide post-secondary education. Few education services are provided directly, although some states operate vocational training institutions and special schools.

The direct service activities of states allow them to utilize a number of policy and program tools. For example, states can directly operate programs for literacy enhancement for special populations, especially those that are already under the care of the state. In many states, for example, a new emphasis has been placed on literacy in the prisons. With institutional populations, of course, the "reach" problem is solved. Motivating people to participate may still be difficult, despite the combination of incentives and punitive actions that can be taken to motivate prisoners or others to seek additional education. Virginia's "No Read, No Release" program is perhaps the most stark example of direct service provision to institutional populations.

A number of states have begun to provide literacy training as part of correctional programs. Besides Virginia's program, for example, South Carolina's Department of Corrections utilizes volunteers to tutor about 1,600 inmates as a supplement to its in-prison education program. Illinois mandates a ninety-day education program for any inmates who have math and reading skills below a sixth grade achievement level.

In many other state-run direct service programs, workers are in frequent contact with clients, making it easier to reach people, motivate them to seek literacy, and recruit them for other service programs. Social service workers in child welfare and public assistance systems have long fulfilled this role, if only to a limited extent. State policies can be developed to ensure that every client of directly provided social service or income maintenance programs is given an opportunity to seek additional literacy skills.

The unemployment insurance (UI) program offers additional possibilities as a tool in reaching out to target groups that the governor has identified as crucial to success of economic development strategies. From UI program data we can identify the long-term unemployed and, to a limited degree, assess their current literacy skills. The job service is also a potential resource in identifying those who need literacy enhancement, and in fact, their referrals to job training programs often fulfill this function now.

Several states have begun experimenting with ways to utilize the unemployment insurance system to assess the need for literacy assistance and offer help. In Tennessee, for example, the interviewers and counselors in local employment security offices use special guides to help identify clients who may need additional literacy skills. In addition, the agency has developed workshops on how to help identity and encourage clients who could benefit from adult basic education or literacy tutoring. In Vermont, unemployment checks are accompanied by cards recruiting unemployed individuals for literacy training.

Institutions of higher education across the country have implemented remedial programs that impart higher level literacy skills to high school graduates who are not ready for college. Although there is much debate about the appropriateness of these programs in a college environment, they are a direct service provided by the state that could be expanded. Colleges with open enrollment, especially those traditionally serving minority students, already provide a great deal of literacy education. These programs could be expanded.

Natural resources agencies have also been enlisted in the effort to enhance literacy for employment. Thirty-eight states or cities have begun programs resembling the Civilian Conservation Corps to employ young people for work in parks, on recreation sites, and for improving the urban landscape. In many of these programs, literacy training is an integral part of the experience. In the Michigan Civilian Conservation Corps program, for example, literacy training and adult basic education are provided as part of the work experience, although time spent on these tasks amounts to only about four hours per week.

INDIRECT SERVICE PROVISION

Most adult education programs operate through grant funding, per-pupil funding, or other support from the state and federal government. These services are provided through local school districts, community colleges, junior colleges and in community-based settings. State and federally financed adult education programs provide basic skills, produce large numbers of people qualifying for the GED and teach thousands of English as a second language courses. State grants to libraries and small seed grants to volunteer groups have also helped to stimulate the provision of basic literacy services through private, voluntary programs. The great majority of current governmental efforts in addressing adult literacy is provided through the financing mechanism of state governments.

A broad array of governmental programs can be used in reaching the target groups identified by the governor. Any of these programs can be expanded through greater funding and can — to an extent — be directed to serve additional groups. Several possibilities of re-targeting resources or expanding services among these programs include:

Adult Basic Education: The federally supported adult education program is the largest provider of literacy training in the country. In 1985, over 2.8 million adults were enrolled in adult education, a sixfold increase in an eighteen-year period. Despite the large numbers of persons served by adult education programs, they constitute only a small percentage — about six percent — of the nearly 52 million adults the Office of Adult Education considers its "target population." Eligibility for the program is broad: anyone sixteen years of age or older without a high school education may enroll. About 80 percent of enrollees who received twelve hours of instruction or more in 1985 were less than forty-five years old and slightly more women than men participated in the program. Whites constituted 37 percent of the enrollment, while blacks and Hispanic participants accounted for 18 percent and 31 percent of enrollees respectively. Over 850,000 enrollees were limited-English-speaking adults.

Most adult education programs provide instruction in the classroom environment, although increasing numbers of programs are using individualized instructional methods, computer and other telecommunications technologies, and methods that allow education to be delivered outside the classroom. Program providers include a wide variety of institutions such as high schools, community colleges, and community-based organizations. The adult education system, a structure that has developed over the past twenty years, provides an important resource for policymakers seeking to expand services funded by state government.

Adult Vocational Education: Adult vocational and technical education programs are extensive and provided through vocational and technical schools, community colleges, junior colleges as well as by the private sector. About one-third to one-half of state vocational education funds are expended for training adults. Training ranges from the most basic job skills to highly technical courses leading to an associate degree. Depending on the target for literacy enhancement, resources invested in these programs can be directed at enhancing literacy as a part of the training process. In addition, combined adult basic education and skills training programs can offer both literacy education and job-related education as part of a multi-year program.

JTPA : Under the Job Training Partnership Act (JTPA), Private Industry Councils are currently able to provide basic skills, including literacy enhancement, in order to prepare unemployed people for skills training leading to jobs. Basic skills and literacy improvement skills are provided under all titles of JTPA, including Title II-A for the disadvantaged, Title II-B (summer programs), Title III for dislocated workers and Title IV (national programs including the Job Corps and other programs targeted to Indian and Native Americans, immigrants and seasonal farm workers, and veterans). Under the 8 percent set-aside provisions of JTPA, Governors have substantial flexibility in using JTPA funds to provide literacy training to youth and adults, dropout prevention services, and school-to-work transition programs.

Under the JTPA program, literacy training can be provided by community groups, private vocational training schools, community colleges, the private sector, and other groups. Governors have a special set-aside fund under the JTPA program that can be used creatively to help bring together other sources of literacy training funds as long as the literacy training can be linked directly to private sector jobs.

JTPA funds are relatively flexible and the program is oriented toward measurable objectives, primarily job placement. This focus, however, means that most JTPA programs are concerned with specific job training and tend to address literacy as a preparation for skill training rather than as a major focus. In addition, some have observed that the emphasis on job placement rates encourages JTPA programs to seek clients with the best basic skills available rather than those who need extensive help in improving literacy.

For a governor, JTPA funds can be used to help knit together other services through the flexibility of govenors' set-aside funds. JTPA programs already provide many basic education services which can be expanded as part of the tools available to a governor in developing programs to enhance literacy.

Community Services Block Grant (CSBG) and Social Services Block Grant Programs: These programs also provide mechanisms to reach large numbers of social services providers who serve many of the same people that adult literacy efforts will likely be designed to reach. CSBG funds already sponsor many community-based adult education and literacy programs. These mechanisms provide an opportunity for targeting existing resources to the problem and for reaching into low-income communities in stimulating additional service providers.

VISTA: Vista has recently announced a new program of literacy volunteers who will work in low-income communities to teach literacy and organize community responses to the literacy problem.

Combined Funds: In several states, programs have been implemented that combine funds flowing from adult basic education, JTPA, and social services programs to provide basic literacy skills and help people get jobs. In California, for example, the Greater Avenues to Independence (GAIN) program integrates adult schools, JTPA programs, and county welfare departments in a system designed to upgrade the literacy skills of welfare recipients and the unemployed and to place them in jobs. Michigan's MOST (Michigan Opportunity and Skills Training) program takes a similar approach for public assistance recipients, referring those who need basic literacy skills to appropriate literacy agencies or adult basic education services. The Department of Social Services in Michigan purchases services to meet the individual needs of recipients and their families.

Library Programs: State library systems have been a major source of inspiration for policy development in adult literacy enhancement efforts. Through small grant programs or through the leadership of the state library, a number of states have enlisted the resources and enthusiasm of library personnel in promoting literacy.

Since libraries are a natural focus for volunteer-based literacy efforts, states have begun to utilize their library systems as a way of reaching a broad group of citizens needing literacy help. Libraries all over the country have responded to this challenge in a variety of innovative ways. In South Carolina, for example, the library system maintains and circulates resource materials for literacy volunteers, provides space for tutors and students, publicizes the availability of literacy services and sponsors county and regional literacy coordinators based in libraries. In Alaska, the library system sponsors a "Parents and Tots Reading Program" in which parents learn to read with the help of tutors and then read to their children at library-sponsored sessions.

Other Grant-Funded or Purchased Service Programs: In addition to these major programs currently delivering adult education and job training, it might be possible to utilize other purchase of service or indirect funding systems to address adult literacy enhancement, particularly to recruit people who might use a variety of literacy services. Day care, juvenile justice, mental health, alcohol and drug abuse programs, and other indirectly provided services can be scrutinized for inclusion in an adult literacy initiative.

If the governor's priority is helping parents read to their children, day care programs can be used to identify parents of preschool children with reading deficiencies and refer them to adult literacy services. In Nevada, for example, the Nevada Literacy Coalition plans to provide literacy services to parents of children attending Headstart preschool programs as well as parents using services at public hospital maternity wards. The design of Kentucky's Parent and Child Education (PACE) program envisions a system in which parents of three- and four-year-olds attending preschool will be able to attend small adult education classes to gain basic skills and possibly earn a GED. PACE also offers parents the opportunity to work with their children in the preschool, helping them to learn to be better teachers at home.

Within the juvenile justice system, dropouts and others with educational deficits can be identified and taught basic skills. Indeed, many juvenile programs, both institutional and non-institutional, contain educational elements. Other programs that interact intensively with adults who might have learning or educational deficits can be used at least to identify and perhaps motivate them to seek literacy help. Mental health, alcohol, and drug abuse programs might be asked to identify those in particular target groups for literacy training. Maternal and child health programs, which serve many teenage dropouts and others with limited educational outlooks, could be enlisted in this effort as well.

Many of these programs rely on expertise residing outside the state government system. Services are purchased from volunteer-administered programs, from community-based programs, and from local governments, and are operated in conjunction with the private, for-profit sector. Programs address the gamut of needs from basic skills to English-as-a-second-language to particular vocational training. All of these programs are funded through state agencies and the funding carries with it requirements for program activities. While it would probably be infeasible to add an educational component to each program, the process of reaching out and helping to motivate adults for literacy assistance could be grafted onto the original purposes of these programs fairly easily.

CONDITIONING BENEFITS AND EMPLOYMENT

Inherent in virtually all of the services offered by state government are a series of eligibility requirements and conditions for the receipt of benefits. Although many of these requirements are mandated by the federal government, state governments have considerable latitude to condition the receipt of benefits or services. In addition, state government employs large numbers of people, and within civil rights and other strictures, the conditions of employment are largely left to the discretion of state officials.

An approach to enhancing adult literacy skills being considered or experimented with in a number of states is to condition human services benefits or employment on participation in adult education classes, tutoring, or other literacy-related programs. In Arizona, for example, the governor proposed that AFDC (Aid to Families with Dependent Children) benefit increases be made available only to welfare recipients who enrolled in adult education classes or were employed. A number of other states are building into their "workfare" programs requirements that underskilled recipients enroll in basic literacy or occupational literacy programs. Some of these policies are voluntary, but many are not.

In Missouri, for example, Governor Ashcroft has proposed a "Learnfare" program in which AFDC parents who have not completed high school would be required to register for adult basic education/GED programs, followed by mandatory registration in job skills and job search programs. Availability of day care and other support services would be expanded under this proposed $6 million program.

It would be possible, although not necessarily desirable, to condition a variety of other state benefits on enrollment in adult education or other literacy enhancing programs. In some cases, imposing such a condition might be counterproductive. Since job search is a condition for unemployment benefits, for example, requiring people who receive extended benefits to seek additional education would probably be contradictory. Requiring enrollment in literacy programs for those below certain skill levels for entry into scarce low-income housing, however, might be possible. Needless to say, setting these kinds of requirements for access to health services would be both unethical and impractical.

Another possible "condition setting" policy for state government would be to use the availability of jobs in state government or other state-regulated institutions as a means to offer incentives to people to seek literacy training. North Carolina, for example, has considered whether or not it should refuse to hire young people who have dropped out of school and are seeking no further education. Since jobs in the transportation department, in the parks, and in maintaining state buildings are considered relatively desirable for low-skilled workers, some state officials believe that denying these jobs to young people who have dropped out would give them an incentive to stay in school or return to school.

Although no states have conditioned state or local employment on seeking literacy enhancement, some have begun voluntary programs for state employees. In Virginia, for example, each state agency has been directed by the Governor to establish a literacy referral system for state employees.

Finally, some state officials have considered making school completion or enrollment in an educational program the condition for receiving a driver's license. This policy would be aimed at young people age sixteen to eighteen who have dropped out of school or who are considering dropping out.

All of these possible policies involving setting conditions on benefits or privileges presume that incentives or disincentives are necessary to induce people to seek additional education or enhance literacy. They also presume that the supply of literacy training programs or adult education classes can be expanded to fulfill the demand created by the application of the incentives. These are large and untested assumptions. Nevertheless, these examples illustrate the ways in which state government could influence the behavior of individuals who are assumed to need additional literacy skills.

USING THE TAX SYSTEM

Like other systems operated by state government, the tax system could be used to influence the behavior of both individuals and firms in seeking and providing literacy services. Although the tax incentives have been reduced in the federal tax system, many states still utilize income, sales, and property tax incentives to address a broad range of issues. Property tax circuit breakers limit the tax burden on senior citizens; sales tax exemptions promote the sale of farm equipment and reduce tax burdens on farmers; and a variety of other tax expenditures are designed to attract industry, create jobs, promote research and development, and influence a host of other activities.

It might be possible to consider using the state tax system to provide incentives both to employers and individuals for literacy enhancement. In several states, for example, providing a tax credit to employers that provide adult basic education or GED programs at the workplace have been considered. At least one state has considered providing an income tax credit to individuals who receive a GED or achieve other measurable adult basic education credentials.

Providing tax incentives for businesses to provide or arrange literacy training might be targeted to firms which face adjustment problems or the probability of generating a large number of displaced workers. Tax credits for providing on-the-job training could be expanded to include a wider range of literacy training as well as specific job training. Incentives for individuals could be tied to the achievement of GEDs or other measurable movement along the literacy continuum. Just as many teachers are automatically rewarded for achieving masters degrees, for example, the tax system could enable employers to raise salaries of workers without high school diplomas once they had achieved them.

In looking at the tax system and its incentives, however, care must be taken to make sure that tax expenditures are targeted to the appropriate people and firms. Compared to federal taxes, state taxes are relatively low. As a result, large percentage tax breaks must be offered in order to induce people or firms to act. In addition, tax credits or exemptions must be tied to measurable, easily confirmed behavior and, therefore, may not be amenable to the field of literacy, where progress is difficult to measure. Tax incentive programs tied to specific outcomes, such as GEDs or occupational certification of one kind or another may skew the response of the private sector toward those outcomes.

Tax incentives may also be relatively inefficient, at least at the start. In one analysis undertaken for a governor, the possibility of awarding a $500 per person income tax credit for achievement of a GED was explored. Since the state already awarded about 11,000 GEDs per year without the tax credit, state officials knew that the immediate cost of the program would be at least $5.5 million without inducing any change in individual or corporate behavior. Nevertheless, the tax system can be considered as part of a policy mix in which the issue of incentives for individuals and firms is being addressed.

Another use of the tax system could be to substitute one kind of tax for another in directing revenue streams toward literacy or other job training activities. Just such a program is underway in California. Under this program, firms are allowed to pay a small percentage of their unemployment insurance tax toward a special fund for retraining current workers. The idea is to divert funds that would otherwise be spent for UI benefits into preventive retraining activities, including literacy enhancement.

INFLUENCING PRIVATE ENTERPRISE

States regulate private economic activities in a variety of ways, including business permitting; enforcing environmental regulations; applying workplace safety rules; and direct regulation of utilities, banks, and insurance companies. In terms of application to adult literacy efforts, states can survey their business regulation activities to ensure that regulatory barriers to firms and employees are not erected when the private sector seeks to provide literacy services.

The most important role in relation to the private sector, however, will likely lie in the area of stimulating the private sector to provide literacy services. While many large firms, such as IBM, already exert considerable effort in providing literacy and skills training, others might be encouraged to do so by state government. In addition, some states have extensive private vocational school systems and other private educational institutions that might be stimulated to seek out those in need of literacy services and to provide help.

The Business Council for Effective Literacy has been working with many companies to identify how the private sector can cooperate with state and local governments to enhance literacy. Businesses are urged to make grants to local adult literacy programs, provide in-kind assistance, help develop new technologies and approaches to instruction, strengthen statewide literacy coalitions and volunteer groups and support research and data gathering about the extent of the problem.

The most important role for the private sector, according the the Business Council, is to set up employee basic skills programs in the workplace or in the community. In Denver, for example, Honeywell and other electronics, light manufacturing, and service firms provide job-specific English and reading instruction to recent immigrants. Consolidated Edison provides extensive literacy and adult education opportunities for its New York City employees. The

Florida Steel Corporation permits employees to enroll in an in-plant program which offers basic skills training for people who read at less than an eighth grade level and GED review for those without a high school diploma. Throughout the country, businesses are expanding training and literacy programs in the workplace. An important role for state government is to stimulate and encourage private firms to expand such programs.

One way that states could carry out this role would be by instituting a voucher system for the purchase of literacy enhancement services. States could provide literacy vouchers to certain groups or to firms that would help pay for literacy services leading to measurable improvements in adult literacy. These vouchers or certificates would be available to individuals, who could then look either to the private sector or the public sector for literacy assistance. The vouchers could be tied directly to performance; vouchers would not "turn into money" until individuals had demonstrated a desired literacy performance level. The effect of a voucher system would be to stimulate development of a broad range of small businesses providing literacy enhancement services. Voucher systems could also be designed with a matching feature, to encourage even small firms to help pay for literacy assistance. At the same time, the state could utilize its regulatory and consumer protection functions to ensure that private educational institutions had adequate facilities and programs before the vouchers could be used for their programs.

LICENSING INDIVIDUALS

In addition to regulating firms, states license individuals for a broad range of occupations and activities. Occupational licensing – which sets standards for education and qualifications for occupations ranging from barbers and beauticians to doctors and lawyers – is an important regulatory function directed at individuals. States also license the driving of motor vehicles; hunting and fishing; and the provision of child care, foster care, and health care services. In addition, the new immigration law involves essentially "licensing" formerly illegal immigrants for continued presence in the country. Although the federal government is the "licenser" in this case, there will be close cooperation between federal, state, and local authorities in trying to meet the educational and social service needs of this population.

One approach, although a questionable one, to utilizing the occupational licensing system would be to encourage licensing boards to include the assessment of literacy skills during the licensing process and raise standards for those occupations where low literacy skill levels are now required. Depending on the occupational licensing standards currently in place, this policy might have the effect of raising some literacy levels but might also unnecessarily restrict entry into occupations by low income persons, immigrants, and others who are likely to have educational deficits.

Another way to utilize the licensing systems of states for enhancing adult literacy would be to take advantage of the fact that they are a major point of contact with the public. Using these points of contact, literacy assessment and referral to literacy programs might be possible. In Arizona, for example, officials are exploring the use of the driver's license test as a screening mechanism for persons with low literacy skills. Since the driver's examination is given both in written form and orally, officials reason that persons requesting the oral examination might need additional literacy training. By identifying these people and offering them literacy services, Arizona may be able to influence large numbers of people, especially young adults, to seek literacy enhancement. Similar policies could be applied to other licensing procedures (although applying literacy measurement to hunting and fishing licenses might be a good way to start a recall petition aimed at the governor).

INFLUENCING LOCAL GOVERNMENT

Despite resistance from nearly all locally elected officials, states mandate a host of requirements on local governments, including counties, cities, school districts, library districts and many other special districts. In a few states, legislatures have required of themselves that state mandates must be accompanied by state funds, but for the most part states still exercise the power to mandate local activities with or without appropriations to cover the costs.

States could require various levels of local government to assist in the job of enhancing literacy. Local governments could be required to assess the literacy of their employees and provide literacy training. School districts could be required to offer literacy training to parents of preschool children or parents of children in elementary schools. Alternative high schools could be mandated for large school districts to attract recent dropouts back into school. States could require various levels of local governments to provide literacy services as a condition for receiving a variety of seemingly unrelated aid, most of which is loosely tied to community or economic development. These grants cover not only the social services but also assistance in water and sewer construction, building and maintaining highways, supporting recreation and housing opportunities. States could also condition local eligibility for industrial revenue bonds and other forms of financing on demonstration of action concerning adult literacy.

These are extreme examples. Few states are likely to link disparate aid streams to adult literacy enhancement efforts, nor are they likely simply to mandate the provision of literacy services by local governments. Nevertheless, more subtle mandates are possible as are inducements to local governments to address the problem.

In encouraging local responses, states should identify barriers that prevent local governments and special districts from assessing needs and providing literacy services. With the financial strictures currently placed on local governments, for example, most local officials will be hard-pressed to respond to encouragement by the state or the public. State officials can help local governments provide resources to schools, libraries and other local institutions to provide literacy services. In Virginia, for example, the state legislature recently enacted a law allowing school districts to levy one-tenth of a mill in property taxes for adult literacy efforts. Kentucky has provided funds to each county government with the requirement that these funds be spent, generally, to combat illiteracy.

PROVIDING LEADERSHIP

State government can also provide leadership for citizens and firms in addressing the issue of adult literacy. The governor can focus attention on the issue; the legislature can create commissions and commission studies; state officials can make the issue a high priority in speeches, public appearances, media campaigns and through the use of other communication techniques. The governor can call together leaders of the private sector to support volunteer efforts and explore ways in which businesses can enhance literacy among employees.

To date, the leadership role has been the primary response of governors and other state officials in addressing the issue of adult literacy. Recent media campaigns, especially ABC/PBS's Project Literacy U.S. (PLUS), have focused public attention on the issue. Books such as Jonathan Kozol's *Illiterate America* have made strident pleas for dramatic action to combat illiteracy. Citizen groups have been formed and volunteer coalitions have sprung up all over America.

In a recent survey of governors' offices, the Council of State Policy & Planning Agencies has found that governors are exerting this leadership role primarily by creating and sometimes funding coalitions of groups concerned with adult literacy. Of twenty-nine responses, twenty-three states had created literacy coalitions. In most cases, these coalitions have been initiated by the governor. In a few cases, legislatures have passed legislation authorizing coalition activities and providing funds for their operation.

The survey explored the goals and responsibilities of gubernatorially supported literacy coalitions. These include:

- Increase public awareness of the adult literacy problem and possible remedies;
- Facilitate the coordination of adult literacy services across the state;
- Collect information on the extent of the state's illiteracy problem;
- Mobilize private/public funding for adult literacy;
- Encourage the development of regional or local literacy coalitions and programs;
- Provide a clearinghouse for adult literacy information and technical assistance to local programs;
- Encourage participation of target groups in programs and help recruit tutors; and,
- Develop a long-range statewide literacy plan.

Most literacy coalitions have started since 1985, although a few were created in 1983 and 1984. Coalitions have broad memberships, usually including representatives of business and industry, unions, community organizations, volunteer literacy groups, state and local agencies, and the media. Most coalitions have developed strong public awareness and outreach campaigns, including speeches, proclamations such as "adult literacy months," local and cable TV programs and toll-free hotlines for literacy assistance and volunteer help.

In their short lives, state literacy coalitions have also been very active in performing the information clearinghouse function. Coalitions have established literacy resource centers, developed directories of existing state literacy resources, developed newsletters, encouraged the development of local and regional networks of literacy providers and produced training manuals. Coalitions have also pressed for increased state funding for literacy initiatives. In Arkansas, for example, the Governor supported an appropriation of $2.8 million for adult literacy improvements as part of the efforts surrounding the creation of the coalition.

Literacy coalitions have also organized nationally. At least 15 have banded together to share information on literacy enhancement strategies and to work with groups such as the National Association of State Boards of Education, the National Governors' Association, and other national organizations interested in policies to enhance literacy.

The existence of literacy coalitions testifies to the fact that governors believe that adult literacy is a serious issue. It also indicates that most governors and state officials do not have firm policies and strategies in mind for pursuing the issue, since much of the planning and proposing of literacy policies has been, in effect, delegated to the literacy coalitions.

In addition to creating literacy coalitions, leadership opportunities include using a variety of communications techniques to increase public awareness of the problem, promote local and volunteer efforts to enhance literacy and stimulate the private sector to contribute to the solution. Project Literacy US (PLUS) has not only aired national television programs focusing on the issue of adult literacy but also maintains state-by-state contacts who work to promote awareness of the issue and constructive responses in every state. Television stations, radio stations, newspapers, and book publishers have joined in the public awareness campaign.

The media has also contributed to literacy training. In Detroit, for example, WXYZ television has developed a literacy television series called "Learn to Read" which is being aired by over forty ABC affiliates. The Detroit News also produced and printed worksheets corresponding to the daily instructional broadcasts.

Governors have used the "bully pulpit" to call attention to the issue of adult literacy in state after state. In 1987, over thirty State of the State or budget messages at least mentioned the problem of adult literacy.

State officials have also used their influence to convene business and union leaders to address the issue. A major element of the Michigan Adult Literacy Initiative, for example, is the creation of local and regional public/private partnerships. Through such groups, General Motors and the UAW are conducting a literacy assessment program in local schools. The UAW/Ford Basic Skills Enhancement Program provides in-plant instruction on a variety of literacy skills as well as referral to community educational programs. Supported by the Governor, the Vermont Alliance for Adult Literacy has been assisted by community groups and businesses alike in organizing volunteer literacy efforts. Businesses have contributed space, developed model training programs for employees, and offered financial support.

In the effort to exert leadership and focus public awareness on the problem of adult literacy, governors are not alone. State chief school officers, community college presidents, higher education officials and others are attempting to rally support to address the issue. Since education officials have long considered adult education as one of their primary responsibilities, some governors have been careful to include education leaders and other publicly elected officials in literacy awareness efforts. In some cases, governors have assigned the task of leading literacy coalitions to other high elected officials, such as Lieutenant Governors or Chief State School Officers.

Leadership need not be confined to exhortation but can also involve example. State government can set an example for the private sector by implementing adult literacy assessment and literacy skills training within its own workforce. States can also urge local governments to do so. States can also implement incentive pay plans, for example, that reward workers for upgrading literacy skills and obtaining GEDs and other educational credentials. Many states help pay tuition for professional employees seeking additional education. This practice can be extended to non-professional staff in offices and throughout the state personnel system. Staff serving state institutions, road maintenance workers, and others can be offered incentives and help in obtaining new skills. State workers can also be urged to read to their children and can be provided with materials to help them do so. As major employers, state governments can implement workplace literacy programs in order to upgrade their own workforces and as an example to large private employers.

Policymakers searching for strategies to address the issue of adult literacy will want to assess the full range of state government powers as well as the leadership opportunities available to encourage the private sector, non-profit organizations, and citizen volunteers to assist the enhancing literacy. From this assessment, policy planners can develop options for the governor's consideration that involve all the resources available to him, not just the traditional programs aimed at the problem. With this larger arsenal, the governor will have a better chance of articulating a coherent strategy to address a very large and complex problem.

Because of the size and complexity of the problem, the definitional issues and the need for targeting, policy strategies must be broadly conceived but their results must be specific and measurable. Otherwise, adult literacy policy may become merely an amalgam of public awareness efforts and incremental additions to the current literacy delivery system. While both these elements will no doubt be important to the development of any strategy, alone they are not likely to do the job of enhancing literacy for jobs and productivity.

The governor's policymaking process is the focal point where all the diverse opportunities for state action to address adult literacy can be merged into a unified and effective policy. Yet there will be limits on the governor, just as state actions are limited. In Chapter 6, we will discuss the specifics of how a governor might exert leadership within state government and on a larger stage to address the issue.

Chapter 4 Notes

1. Lewis Perelman, *Technology and Transformation of Schools, Public Education Strategies for a More Competitive Nation*, (Washington, D.C.: National School Boards' Association, March, 1987), 71 - 73.
2. David Harman, *Illiteracy: A National Dilemna*, (New York: The Cambridge Book Company, 1987), 50 - 51.

PROGRAMS TO IMPROVE ADULT LITERACY: THE STATE OF THE ART

INTRODUCTION

This chapter of the policy guide provides a framework for policymakers to spur the development of adult literacy programs that work. It is also designed to enable policymakers to evaluate the efficacy of existing programs and to estimate the potential of those already in the planning stage.

The issue of sponsorship or aegis of program operation often begins most discussions of program options for adult literacy. Policy options are thus framed around an assessment of what exists in the state in the form of programs, legislation, and financing. These summaries provide a good understanding of financial resources available to support literacy programs and organizations or groups that have had experience in providing services, but they provide the state policymaker little information about what works in what circumstances. The result of this approach is to get more of the same or to fill in apparent gaps in service, but not to address the fundamental issue of what works.

To date, no one at the national or state levels has quantified the efficacy of the full range of approaches to upgrading literacy skills. Within specific areas of program sponsorship, some evaluations have attempted to measure progress or improvement by participants. Perhaps the best known of these is the work done by Thomas Sticht in evaluating the military approach.[1] In addition, local programs frequently attempt to measure performance of their participants. Many programs measure success by the number of persons completing the program or course or the number of persons reached through the program. Others use the number obtaining an alternative high school credential as a measure of program performance.[2] No definitive studies have been done which start from the question: "What are we trying to teach and why?" Few studies compare the effects of various methods in achieving that goal.

In the absence of adequate evaluative data which would identify for policymakers the appropriate strategies for improving adult literacy, proxies must be used. A review of the literature provides valuable insights, suggestions, and direction for how to proceed. This chapter organizes this information as responses to a logical series of questions that a policymaker would ask in designing a program that works.

In order to inform the policymaking process, we must first ask the question, *What are we trying to teach and why?* In order to be able to judge the effectiveness of methods to improve literacy skills, one must first clearly state the goal of the intervention. Simply stating that the goal is to improve literacy is not sufficient. Since literacy is best defined contextually, one must also specify what skills are to be imparted or improved for what purpose.

The second question then becomes, *Who are we trying to teach?* As discussed in Chapter 3, state policymakers must be clear about the target groups they are trying to reach. After deciding on the types of skills to be taught and the reason for teaching them, attention must be focused on identifying the groups of individuals who require this type of assistance. In short, designing an effective program or policy intervention requires clarity about the desired outcomes and the people that we are trying to help achieve those outcomes.

After determining what is to be imparted to whom and why, we must then ask, *How should the information be conveyed?* This question begins to focus on the relationship between the learner and the subject matter. While policymakers may be tempted initially to relegate decisions about this level of detail to program managers, they should think again. Experience garnered in operating literacy programs provides valuable policy direction that should be considered and incorporated into overall design. This perspective may be missed if policymakers choose not to focus on questions of program design as they relate to state policy.

A fourth question for policymakers to ask in designing an adult literacy improvement program that works is, *Who should convey the information?* That is, what are the necessary skill levels, training, and background of the instructors that seem to be important to program success? Are there special skills or techniques to aid instructors that seem to make a difference in achieving the desired outcomes of a program?

Finally, policymakers must ask, *How do we know that the skills have been learned?* This is an essential and often unattended element of program design that must be addressed in order to judge whether or not the goals of the governor's policy are being met. Being able to answer this question will also permit state policymakers to make corrections in policy design if the governor's goals are not being reached.

These, then, are the essential questions that must be addressed by state policymakers in designing an effective adult literacy strategy:

- What are we trying to teach and why?
- Who are we trying to teach?
- How should the information be conveyed?
- Who should convey the information?
- How do we know that the skills have been learned?

The issue of sponsorship, or how the program should be supported and financed, thus becomes one of implementation rather than design and should not be addressed until after the questions of design have been answered.

HISTORY

Programs to enhance literacy outside the schools have a long history in America. Literacy education was provided by ethnic groups to hasten the transition to full participation in the economy. For example, the Jewish and Italian communities as well as those of other nationalities provided English language education to immigrants. These literacy improvement activities were privately sponsored and community-based. Other private volunteer programs were created through private philanthropy designed to teach illiterate English-speaking persons to read and write. During World War II, the military also began implementing programs to reduce illiteracy.

In the 1960s, the lack of literacy skills in the population became a national concern. Since that time, a broad mix of public and private efforts to improve the level of literacy of the United States population has developed. Three major pieces of legislation in that decade set the national stage for addressing adult literacy. The first two focused on literacy in the context of job preparation and readiness.

The Manpower Development and Training Act of 1964 was enacted to provide job training for the unemployed. It was later amended to provide basic education skills because such a large percentage of the participants were found to be functionally illiterate. This legislation was followed by the Economic Opportunity Act of 1964 which provided the first grants to states for literacy programs, also workforce-oriented. The thrust of these initiatives was entirely on preparation for employment. In 1966, the Adult Education Act was enacted to provide basic education and literacy skills for adults, not necessarily linked to a specific employment goal.

Private, nonprofit, volunteer-based programs were also gearing up at this time. In 1968, U.S. church groups organized into the National Affiliate for Literacy Advance, building on the international work of Laubach in teaching basic reading and writing skills to people in underdeveloped countries. This group became Laubach Literacy Action in 1978. Another volunteer literacy effort was formalized in the late '60s as Literacy Volunteers of America (LVA). Inspired by Laubach's work, Ruth Colvin, herself a reading specialist, built on Laubach's individual tutoring approach, and developed more formalized tutor training materials.

In the private for-profit sector, the first in-house literacy programs also began about the same time with the Polaroid education program. Polaroid's original program focused on high school math and chemistry. In the late 1960s and early '70s, Graduate Equivalency Degree (GED), adult basic education (ABE), and English as a Second Language (ESL) programs were added for Polaroid employees.[3]

Since that time, adult literacy programs have sprung up across the country. In addition to the ABE programs and those run by the military, other major literacy programs offered by the public sector include those programs funded under the Job Training Partnership Act, those provided through the vocational education system in the states and those operated through the library systems. In addition to LVA and Laubach Literacy, The Coalition for Literacy and The Business Council for Effective Literacy were organized to foster private sector awareness of the need for and efforts to address the issue of upgrading the level of literacy in the workforce. Private for-profit sector programs for the workforce abound, sponsored by a broad array of companies including Planters Peanuts, Aetna, American Institute of Banking, The Seafarers International Union, McGraw-Hill, Inc., and J.P. Stevens Company.

In recent years, the number and diversity of literacy programs have grown. The largest single source of funds for literacy is the ABE program, but significant funds are also expended through the Job Training Partnership Act and the Vocational Rehabilitation Act. In addition, an increasing number of states are allocating state funds for literacy enhancement.

Literacy improvement programs are sponsored by governments, volunteers, community groups, private businesses, and coalitions of interested parties. They are operated by schools, state and local governments, the military, volunteers, community-based organizations, other not-for-profit organizations, and private businesses. Programs also vary by the aspect of literacy they are trying to teach, their methods of instruction, the type and skills of teachers used, and by many other factors such as methods of testing and assessment, instructional material, and the extent to which success is measured or evaluated. Literacy improvement programs in the U.S. are not a monolithic entity. Despite national misunderstanding that literacy programs are all alike in seeking to make "illiterate" persons "literate", there is wide diversity in these programs that makes comparison and evaluation difficult.

This diversity coupled with the lack of adequate evaluative data creates a difficult situation for state policymakers who are trying to determine what programs work. The contribution this guide makes to state policymaking in the field of adult literacy is that of providing a structure or framework to guide state decision makers in the design of effective policies and programs to improve adult literacy.

WHAT ARE WE TRYING TO TEACH AND WHY?

In order to design a literacy program that works, one must first decide what skills are needed by what portion of the population. The definition of the size and nature of the state's population requiring improved literacy skills, the relationship between a state literacy initiative and other policy goals of the governor, and targeting of the initiative to fulfillment of a larger social and or economic goal must first be determined. As discussed in preceding chapters, the governor must decide the context within which a literacy initiative will be designed. Why do we want to improve literacy? Literacy is not a condition that either exists or does not; rather, it involves a continuum of skills. State policymakers must first clarify their reasons for wanting to improve literacy in order to determine what to teach.

Approaches to Defining "What to Teach"

Historically, literacy improvement efforts have focused on imparting specific and discrete components of knowledge, such as basic reading, writing, and arithmetic; or on the acquisition of skills associated with discrete tasks, such as passing the GED examination or filling out an application form. Other literacy programs have focused on what has been called functional competence, or the capacity to perform in particular circumstances such as on the job, as a consumer, or as a parent. More recently, the changing demands of the workplace suggest that literacy requires a core set of information processing and problem-solving skills, which include basic coding and decoding — skills that are portable. These portable skills can then be applied in different and changing life circumstances.[4]

These basic approaches to literacy improvement, represented by the "discrete components of knowledge" approach and the "portable set of skills" approach are seemingly at right angles to each other. The first cuts literacy vertically, into separable components and the second cuts horizontally, into broader underlying and prerequisite skills. The "functional competency" approach could be envisioned as an application or extension of either. It is used by some as an extension of the "discrete components of knowledge" approach and by others as a way of illustrating the "portable skills" approach.

The "Discrete Components of Knowledge" Approach to Literacy Education

The traditional approach to literacy education has been to teach basic and intermediate coding and decoding, either in an academic or functional context.[5] Reading is one skill; writing is another. History is a separate subject from geography. Health and safety is another body of knowledge. This is the approach that the elementary and secondary school system takes. The assumptions of this approach are that there are blocks of information and knowledge that the learner lacks and that this knowledge can be separated into discrete packages and transferred to the learner. The unstated assumption is that these skills can then be applied by the learner in all aspects of life.

Many literacy programs focus on conveying knowledge associated with these individual or selected aspects of literacy. For example, a program may teach basic reading, basic arithmetic, or basic writing. It may also attempt to improve vocabulary, writing style, communication, and listening skills. Or, it may be focused on teaching English as a Second Language. In each case, there is a specific body of knowledge that can be imparted to the learner.

This approach is used in many programs across the nation; programs that are supported by a wide variety of sponsors in a wide variety of settings. In this approach, programs may vary by the level of skill or knowledge they are attempting to impart and by the extent to which they use materials relevant to the life of the adult learner. They are alike in that they focus on a learner's acquisition of a specific and discrete knowledge base.

What do we know about the success of this approach as applied to adult learners? First, we know that this is the approach most frequently taken in the traditional academic environment of the school system – the environment in which these adult learners have failed to acquire these basic skills.[6]

Second, we know that even individuals with basic coding and decoding skills often lack the ability to function productively in society.[7,8] The assumption that these skills will enable persons to be productive members of today's economy is seriously challenged by the growing concerns of employers and is underscored by results of surveys, such as that performed by the National Assessment for Education Progress (NAEP). The work done by Sticht with the military showed that even if gains were made in the acquisition of discrete bodies of knowledge and skills through this approach to literacy training, within six weeks 80% of those gains are lost unless the skills taught were applied to regular life situations. Losses were still experienced, but minimized if tied to use with practice.[9]

The underlying assumption that the skills acquired by adults through this approach will then be generalized appears to be incorrect in light of the NAEP study of literacy among young adults. This study showed that there was only about a 25% overlap between the ability to read paragraphs and the ability to read and interpret prose. The same was true for overlap of either of these skills with the ability to read and make computations.

Even if an adult were sufficiently motivated to acquire the discrete skills that he or she was unable to acquire in school, the utility of simple acquisition of these skills alone is highly questionable. If employers' demands for workers whose skills enable them to change and adapt to change are valid, the approach of teaching discrete bodies of knowledge and skills to adults may be insufficient for the conditions that most adults will face in the workplace or the broader society.

The "Functional Competency" Approach to Literacy Education

In response to the concern that literacy include the ability to perform certain tasks as well as possess specific bodies of knowledge, many programs focus all or part of their instruction on functional or competency-based education. "Those who plan education programs based on the existing competencies of people look first at what the adult has already learned. They are less interested in whether the new competencies sought by learners have utility within the educational system itself than in whether these competencies are important in the person's life. They encourage people to learn what they need to know rather than simply to pass examinations."[10]

Literacy improvement programs operated by the military are now all competency-based.[11] In the last two decades, the approach of the military has moved away from any focus on basic skills education for its own sake and toward instruction preparing individuals for specific job tasks.[12] Recently, the U.S. Departments of Defense, Education, and Labor decided to jointly demonstrate the application of a competency-based approach to literacy enhancement, expanding on work done in the military. This program, called the Job Skills Education Program, is a computer-based approach to diagnosing job-related literacy and basic skills deficiencies and providing instruction to correct those deficiencies.

Other examples of the functional competency approach can be found in programs which prepare learners for passing the GED or other high school equivalency degree, or for the acquisition of specific skills needed to fill out an application for a job or a drivers license. The focus of instruction in these cases is, however, still on the acquisition of skills associated with a discrete task.

Most literacy improvement programs today build into their curricula opportunities to apply basic skills to problems of daily life.[13] This movement was spurred by the widely reviewed Adult Performance Level (APL) study done in 1975[14], through the University of Texas. This study, as discussed in Chapter Two, focused attention on the need for functional literacy in five areas: occupational knowledge, consumer skills, health and safety, community resources, and government and law. The APL study was not designed to address program operations but many concluded that defining literacy based on performance in life implied designing programs according to functional competencies.

Other competency-based systems of education have been developed. Perhaps most obvious is the California Adult Student Assessment System (CASAS) . CASAS is an instructional management system designed to guarantee that instruction will "help students do those things that are essential to functioning well on the job and in life."[15] CASAS includes a core of twenty-six areas of competency, a list of instructional materials appropriate for each competency area and classified by level, and over two thousand measures of student performance within these areas of competency.

Other examples are found in state and city programs (the New York City Adult Literacy Initiative, the New York State Department of Correctional Services' Adult Functional Competencies Curriculum); labor unions (Consortium for Worker Literacy in New York); and other workforce- and workplace-based programs (Polaroid, NYNEX, Control Data); and, in particular, community-based programs (Barrio Education Project in San Antonio, or Push Literacy Action Now in Washington, D.C.). The list of programs attempting to achieve competency-based behavioral objectives is quite large and growing.

What do we know about the success of these approaches? First, we know that this approach seems to retain more people in the programs than the "discrete components of knowledge" approach.[16,17] Because this approach is more relevant to learners' perceptions of their needs, the retention rate in competency-based programs seems to be higher than in others. While there is widespread debate over the definitions of areas of functional competence and over when they should be built into the curriculum,[18] there does appear to be a growing consensus that a competency-based approach to literacy training is better preparation for adults who wish to move into the mainstream of society.[19,20]

Despite the increased relevance of the competency-based approach to the needs of learners, critics argue that a focus on the acquisition of particular functional skills may not provide adequate training in basic coding and decoding skills. The functional competency approach in its applications is almost always used with persons with *at least* a fourth grade reading level simply because that minimal level of coding and decoding skill is necessary to understand the examples of everyday life situations which adults face.[21] In fact, most materials drawn as examples in everyday life — newspapers, employment materials, etc. — are geared to the eighth grade reading level.[22] Those persons who can survive in society functioning between the fifth and eighth grade reading levels still have enormous reading and other functional deficits. A program that responds only to an adult's request to learn a specific set of occupational skills may neglect important training in basic coding and decoding skills and miss an opportunity to avoid the need for retraining in the future.

Narrowing the field of information to be imparted to specific functional competencies does, however, reduce the instructional time required. While some experts in the field suggest that with traditional methods of instruction about one hundred hours of instruction yields a one-year increase in reading ability, with a functional approach the same gain can be achieved with thirty to thirty-five hours of instruction. [23] The trade-off for policymakers involves the breadth of preparation versus the time required for instruction. Given the large amounts of time required to acquire basic skills, some policymakers opt for narrowing the focus to immediate life situations of the learner, once again optimistically assuming that the learned skills can be generalized into other aspects of life.

Unfortunately, a major criticism of these approaches is that they simply extend the academic or compartmentalized approach to literacy to a broader array of individual and specific tasks, without providing the basic problem-solving skills that would enable the learner to generalize to situations not anticipated in the classroom.[24] For example, teaching an individual to read a bus schedule in order to get to work or teaching an individual how to perform a specific two-step computation in order to function in a new job may solve the immediate problem of getting to work and may be adequate for the job as long as the nature of the job does not change substantially. This type of instruction, though more firmly based in the life requirements of the learner, does not necessarily prepare an individual to perform similar functions like reading a tax table or benefit chart or performing a totally different two-step calculation. That is, the skills learned are not necessarily portable.

The "Portable Skills" Approach to Literacy Education

A very different approach to improving adult literacy skills is based on the assumption that being literate in today's society is not just a function of ability to code and decode or perform separate and discrete tasks, but is rather a function of problem-solving or information-processing skills.[25] The proponents of this approach argue that the knowledge of reading and writing or, for example, of deciphering a bus schedule is not sufficient in and of itself. Rather,

109

the acquisition of skills in such a way as to enable application of the knowledge in varying and changing situations of everyday life is the essential component of literacy in today's society.

The best example of the "portable skills" approach to literacy is reflected in an assessment instrument rather than in a program design. The (NAEP) study of literacy measured literacy skills in young adults in terms of three different aspects of literacy –prose literacy, document literacy, and quantitative literacy (see Chapter Two).[26]

Proponents of adapting this approach to literacy improvement argue that there is a portable set of underlying skills that can be identified and taught and that the learner would be able to generalize these skills in their application to the many and varying aspects of his or her life.[27]

Mikulecky raises a caution here. First, there is a potential problem of falling into the trap of treating the teaching of portable skills in much the same fashion as that embodied by the "discrete components of knowledge" approach. That is, attempting to teach problem-solving skills as a component of an academic curricula rather than providing a broad array of functional examples in which different types of problem-solving skills can be acquired. Second, while several experts in the field have made attempts to identify a core set of needed skills that, when compared, look very much alike (Sticht and NAEP, for example), there may be a vast difference between the logical determination of what is needed and the psychology of the way people learn. Mikulecky suggests that teaching two-step computations, for example, could be as alien to the learner as teaching simple arithmetic or reading in a traditional way. Rather, he recommends teaching many different applications of two-step computations and identifying the similarities in the processes rather than concentrating on the processes themselves. The main focus would be on the applications, exposing the learner to as many and varied experiences as possible.

Mikulecky's conclusions are based on a large body of knowledge about the way in which skills are transferred.[28] He believes that the closer an experience in which skills should be generalized is to a learned experience, the more likely the generalization will take place; the less similar the situation, the less likely that the skill will be generalized. He also suggests that the problem of generalization is much more difficult for less literate persons. Persons who have failed to acquire literacy skills may have the least ability to "stretch" – to apply their skills in other areas. So the problem is compounded. As Edward Hirsh points out, it may be that increased ability to generalize requires an increasingly broad base of knowledge and range of life experiences. Hence, those who are the most literate and the most educated are most capable of generalizing skills. Conversely, those who are the least literate with the smallest base of knowledge and experiences have the least ability to generalize in the application of skills.[29]

Reports from the business community seem to suggest that firms increasingly require workers with a broad variety of skills, abilities, and knowledge.[30] These competencies were defined as language and communication skills, reading, writing, and computational skills that can be applied in varying work settings. The business sector wants persons with skills that can be applied to different and changing workplace demands.[31] This implies a need for problem solving and more complex information processing skills.

The authors of *The Subtle Danger* conclude that "(t)he solution ... is ... to develop, through instructional experimentation, a curriculum that teaches the underlying skills and strategies required by everyday literacy tasks, and to extend this education to non-school agencies: job training, government programs for the unemployed and the poor, television and the like."[32] While this approach is largely theoretical, there are several places where efforts are now being made to translate the "portable skills" approach into curriculum.

Irwin Kirsch, coauthor of the NAEP report, is working at the Educational Testing Service in Princeton, New Jersey, to translate the NAEP assessment tool into curriculum, relying heavily on functional competency applications. Larry Mikulecky at Indiana University is also focusing on teaching general problem solving and information processing skills through the provision of a very broad array of functional competency examples. Sharon Darling, formerly the director of the Adult Education Program in Kentucky, is also working on similar applications of the portable skills approach.

All of these approaches view the use of functional competency applications as essential to teaching a set of portable skills. They specify basic problem solving and information process-ing skills and then use a functional approach to convey them, always being cognizant that the functional applications are just examples of how the underlying skills might be applied.

What do we know about the success of this approach? First, we have no evaluative data on the effectiveness of this approach since it is only now being translated into program content. We do know, however, that this approach appears to hold promise, since it has grown out of experience with the limitations of the "discrete components of knowledge" approach. Many practitioners and schol-ars believe that there is a quantifiable set of "portable" literacy skills that can be conveyed to adult learners and that these skills can be acquired by a learner so that they can be applied to a wide variety of problem-solving and information-processing tasks.[33, 34] The caveat to this approach is that limitations on the ability to generalize may be a function of limited knowledge and life experiences. This suggests that a broad range of functional examples be employed in teaching problem-solving and information-processing skills.

Results from the NAEP and other studies suggest ". . . that primary emphasis on a single aspect of literacy may not lead to the acquisition of the complex information-processing skills and strategies needed to cope successfully with the broad array of tasks adults face."[35] Regardless of the level of literacy on which a state chooses to focus its attention and resources, the best evidence to date strongly suggests that imparting portable skills in a functional context is the best investment that can be made."[36, 37, 38]

State policymakers should *not* assume that one could move others along a continuum, first teaching basic coding and decoding in the traditional way, and then moving to functional competency for intermediate levels of literacy and then on to a higher order of problem-solving skills. Such an approach, while tempting in its appeal to fold in various programs now in operation in the states, is not sound. There is no factual basis on which to assume that such an approach would significantly improve the literacy levels of the adult population. While there is clearly a continuum of literacy skills, approaches to enhancing those skills cannot be viewed as a continuum. In fact, the "portable skills" approach is at direct odds with the "discrete components of knowledge" approach. The "functional competencies" approach can be applied either as an extension of the traditional compartmentalized approach or as a tool to present the context within which the "portable skills" approach can be learned.

Studies also show that basic literacy skills must be used if they are to be retained. [39, 40] An individual may, through the "discrete components of knowledge approach" or even a "functional competencies" acquire a level of literacy sufficient to obtain a job, fill out an application, or even pass the GED or graduate from high school. If those particular skills are not used, however, they will erode. If the skills learned cannot be generalized to different situations, then they will not be used when changes in life circumstances occur. Their erosion is assured. If an individual learns a skill as a generalizable tool to solving problems, either by learning the process of generalization or by learning problem solving in a very broad range of circumstances, then one could expect the skills to be used and retained.

State policymakers must keep in mind, however, the time required to upgrade literacy skills. In the best of circumstances, it now takes an average of eight hundred hours of instruction to move an individual from a second grade to an eighth grade reading level. [41] This is an enormous commitment of time on the part of both the instructor and the learner. It is not surprising that most people in adult literacy programs never finish their course of instruction. In a study of adult literacy program dropouts, Gesela Fitgerald found that many left the program because they found that no real gains were being made for the efforts they were exerting. The learners simply didn't see much hope for a return in terms of improving their life choices. [42]

The answer to the question of what are we trying to teach and why cannot be made unequivocally. Thoughtful observers of adult literacy programs suggest that:

(1) If we attempt to teach reading, writing, arithmetic, and other skills as discrete bodies of knowledge, we run the risk of repeating the failed experience of schooling for many adults. Moreover, the "discrete body of knowledge or skills" approach does not appear to prepare adults for real life experiences or the changing workplace.

(2) Teaching functional competencies is more relevant to "real life" and the job skills needed by adults, but this approach also runs the risk of imparting skills that are quickly outdated or irrelevant to changing circumstances in an adult's life.

(3) An untested but promising approach would take the best elements of the first two approaches and focus them on teaching information-processing and problem-solving skills — skills that could be generalized to changing circumstances at work or at home.

If the economy is changing as rapidly as reported, it may be necessary to use state policies to stimulate this third approach if we are to link successfully literacy enhancement with jobs and productivity.

WHO ARE WE TRYING TO TEACH?

After determining the purpose for which state policymakers wish to improve levels of literacy in their adult population, and what is to be taught in order to best fulfill that purpose, state policymakers should then focus on identifying groups of people who will require this type of intervention in order to meet the state's overall goals. Persons who could benefit from literacy improvement programs can be grouped into categories of like circumstances. They might, for example, be grouped according to their relationship to the workforce:

- Persons needing pre-employment literacy improvement;
- Unemployed persons requiring upgrading of literacy skills in order to become employed;
- Persons requiring English as a Second Language skills in order to obtain and retain employment;
- Employed persons needing higher levels of skills in order to maintain their jobs or advance; and,
- Others requiring improved literacy skills to enhance their quality of life.

Another way to think of the groups of people who might be in need of literacy enhancement skills is by life situation:

- Employed persons seeking to upgrade their skills;
- Workers who have or will be displaced from their jobs

115

for inadequate skills;
- Non-English speaking immigrants;
- AFDC mothers;
- Older workers;
- Out of school teenagers;
- Correctional inmates;
- Handicapped and disabled persons; and,
- Other unemployed adults.

State policymakers will choose target groups based on those that best fit their overall goals. If, for example, a state chooses to focus on upgrading the literacy skills of those not likely to receive services through the private sector but in need of employment, then they might first focus on those persons receiving welfare and unemployment services through state and federal programs.

Subgroupings could then be made in relationship to the workforce. For example, a state might choose to focus on AFDC mothers, unemployed fathers receiving AFDC benefits, persons receiving unemployment benefits and out of school teenagers in AFDC families, juvenile justice programs, and drug and alcohol programs. Within each of these groups, those needing pre-employment skills, reemployment skills and English as a Second Language skills would be identified. These groups and subgroups would then form the target populations for the state.

The Importance of Specifying the Target Groups

Specifying carefully the target groups in an adult literacy effort is important not only to connect policy goals to literacy improvement but also to inform the process of program design. Each of these groups of individuals brings special needs to the learning environment. Programs should be specifically designed to serve a particular target group.[43, 44] They should take into account both the reasons for participating in a program designed to upgrade literacy and the circumstances that may form barriers to attaining that goal. For example, AFDC mothers may wish to improve their literacy in order to obtain employment with some opportunity for advancement and thus move out of a state of dependency. However, transportation to and from the learning site may be difficult to obtain and the need for child care may serve as an obstacle in attending classes. Feelings of isolation and past failures may be difficult to overcome and programs not taking these factors into account will probably experience high drop-out rates.

"Every target group has a half a hundred factors that can sabotage a literacy improvement program," notes Larry Mikulecky. As clearly shown in the NALP (National Adult Literacy Project) study, practitioners in all types of programs have stated that "instruction and learning are hampered by the student's lack of confidence, difficult life situations, and inadequate study skills. Some practitioners believe that learning cannot even take place until the overload of personal problems and some of the resulting psychological blocks to learning are addressed."[45]

While these problems exist for many persons with low level literacy skills, their manifestations may vary considerably depending on life circumstances. For example, the needs of a prisoner working to improve literacy skills in anticipation of parole are quite different from those of a severely handicapped or disabled person or a teenage high school dropout. If these varying needs are not taken into account, the chances of effectively reaching the desired population and retaining them in a literacy improvement program are greatly diminished.[46]

Recruiting the Target Groups

In addition to identifying the target groups to be the focus of the literacy improvement initiative, policymakers must be cognizant of the fact that special efforts must be built into the program design to ensure that persons enrolled in programs are in fact members of that target group. There are two schools of thought about how these groups should be recruited: the self-motivated marketing approach and the targeted outreach approach.

The Self-Motivated Marketing Approach: This approach is based on the assumption that need will drive consumption. In this approach, policymakers specify the state goals for literacy improvement, the required skill levels to be achieved, and a definition of those eligible to participate. Programs are available across the state to which all interested persons can apply. Those eligible persons choosing to participate in the programs become the target group.

This approach assumes that persons who are in need of literacy improvement skills can be made aware of their need, are proximate to services to meet their need, motivated to obtain services to improve their skills, and capable of resolving all obstacles in their path to acquiring those skills. We know that this is rarely the case, particularly for those who fall at the bottom end of the literacy scale. It is true that some programs, particularly English as a Second Language programs and some community-based programs, often have long waiting lists. It is also true that other programs have a very difficult time in finding persons to participate.

While persons are most likely aware of their literacy limitations, the many obstacles between need recognition and skill acquisition may be either real or perceived barriers. A sense of previous failures may have so dampened motivation that obstacles seem insurmountable. The complications of child care, transportation, part time employment, disability, or personal problems may make participation in classes difficult to impossible. Or, an individual may simply see the connection between literacy training and enhanced life options as too tenuous or too time consuming to be worth the effort.

The Targeted Outreach Approach: On the other hand, state policymakers may choose to develop a targeted plan to reach the particular groups identified as candidates for literacy enhancement. This approach takes into account the barriers that individuals within each subgroup may face in taking advantage of literacy improvement programs. State government targets the candidates for literacy improvement through existing government-sponsored or -administered programs, the mass media, or through special public/private sector initiatives.

In this approach, state policymakers also encourage program level outreach, including individual contact, joint plans to remove barriers to participation, and frequent follow-up to prevent dropouts. Contact with individuals is made through existing programs which now serve the target group, neighborhood canvassing, the mass media, public speaking engagements, or word of mouth.

Targeted plans might encourage members of the target group to participate through incentives or exhortation, or might be made mandatory. An incentive approach might, for example, promise early release for prison inmates who acquire basic coding and decoding skills. A mandatory state policy might focus on the teenage dropout population and require that all persons achieve a particular level of basic literacy before they are issued a drivers' license. Another incentive approach might be to provide a tax break for those providing or receiving a literacy improvement credential. (See Chapter 4 for a discussion of incentives.)

The targeted outreach approach assumes that many persons will need assistance in overcoming the barriers to upgrading literacy skills. It pays particular attention to identifying who those persons are, where they are, and what help they will need in order to effectively take advantage of an opportunity to improve their skills.

In summary, there are two major reasons for specifying quite clearly the characteristics of adults state literacy policy is trying to reach: First, identifying the populations to be targeted enables the policymaker to take into account the particular needs, problems, and life circumstances of the learner in approaching the task of improving literacy skills. Programs which remain alert to the changing needs and goals of students and are sensitive to the affective needs of students appear to have greater opportunity for success.[47] Second, a clear identification of the target group enables the policymaker to design specific methods of reaching that group and retaining them in literacy enhancement programs.

HOW SHOULD THE INFORMATION BE CONVEYED?

Within the target groups selected by the governor, both skill levels and motivation of learners will vary considerably. Experience of program operators strongly suggests that these differences be taken into account in designing methods of improving adult literacy.[48]

Much of the literacy improvement curricula that have been developed for adults, particularly instructional approaches to the teaching of reading, are adaptations of materials developed for use in elementary schools. This approach presumes that the learning process of adults is the same as or very similar to that of children. David Harman argues that there is a vast difference in the two; that children are taking their first steps toward literacy whereas adults with low levels of literacy skills have already acquired a level of literacy, albeit an inadequate one. He states that learning in adults has unique attributes that distinguishes it from learning processes during child-hood and adolescence.[49]

Within the adult population, different target groups will approach the learning process from different vantage points. Persons fully literate in another language learning English as a second language will have different needs and expectations than those lacking reading and writing skills in their own language yet seeking English language skill. English-speaking adults interested in obtaining GEDs will have different needs and expectations from a group of displaced workers who read at the level of fourth grade or below.

Adults require attention to their circumstances and a gearing of curriculum to fit their special needs. The NALP study showed that many literacy programs ". . . build strategies aimed at strengthening the student's self-concepts, buttressing their morale and motivation and drawing them out of any feelings of isolation or alienation."[50] According to Hunter and Harman, "adults are motivated to learn that which they see as required or desirable, not what someone tells them is important."[51] Therefore, answering the question of how the information will be conveyed is really a function of three factors:

- What is the existing skill level of the learner and to what level does the learner and the program aspire?
- What is the motivation of the learner; what is the goal for which improved literacy is a tool?
- In what setting and through what methods is the information best conveyed to the learner?

Assessing the Skill and Need Level of Learners

Just as programs must be sensitive to the differences in life circumstances of different target groups, so must they be sensitive to differences in skill levels of learners within each target group. Even a program focused on assisting a particular target group in literacy improvement for a particular purpose must still accommodate vast differences in the skill levels for improvement of the participants.

In order to determine the starting point for each learner, some assessment must be made of his or her position on the literacy continuum. To determine the current level of performance of participants and to ensure proper placement in a class or with instructional materials, most programs use some form of diagnostic testing. These tests are also used throughout the program to assess progress.

All of the programs in the NALP study (225) used diagnostic tests in one form or another. Many programs of business and industry also have individual assessment components designed to help learners diagnose their educational needs. Almost one-third of the NALP programs considered diagnosing the skill level of the learner as the most important component of their program. In most cases, standardized tests were used for initial determination of performance, and less formal methods were used for periodic performance assessments.[52] In a study of community-based literacy programs, while most specified program or learner objectives, "(f)ew, however, have the time and resources to rigorously document and evaluate the results that occur. Some, in fact, prefer to avoid subjecting students to assessment, feeling that it smacks too much of school."[53] Many tutoring programs make no attempt at all to assess entry skill level or measure progress except informally.

Of those who believe in the importance of individual evaluation, there is great debate, however, about the types of tests that should be used to determine initial skill level and to measure progress. Many instructors are skeptical about the ability of standardized achievement tests to measure progress toward the instructional goals they set with learners. Consequently, they are reluctant to present the learner with what they consider an abstract test score that may compound the learners' feelings of inadequacy and failure. There is also the widely held belief that many adult students simply don't test well with conventional testing methods. Many instructors feel that their students have made progress, but they do not know how to capture and quantify that progress.[54]

On the other hand, the use of tests can demonstrate for the instructor and more importantly the learner when an individual is ready to move on. It is important to remember that adult literacy instruction is a means to another end, not an end in itself. "Adult students can and will leave a program if they do not clearly see that their needs are being served and that their time is not being wasted."[55] For those who do well, then, tests help improve self-esteem and self-concept.

The choice of a particular assessment tool is dependent on the decision what to measure. Part of the difficulties experienced by teachers in adapting tests for their use may be due to their lack of clarity about what they and their program are trying to teach and why. To assess appropriately the skill level of the learner upon entry into a literacy improvement program, one must use an instrument designed to assess the kinds of skills the program is trying to teach.

If one is approaching literacy enhancement from the point of view of conveying individual components of literacy, standardized tests are available that can adequately assess skill level. For the traditional academic approach to instruction, many testing instruments exist. Examples of these tests include the California Achievement Test (CAT), the Test for Adult Basic Education (TABE), the Stanford Diagnostic Reading Test and the Wide Range Achievement Test (WRAT). These tests measure the academic literacy level of students.

If a state chooses to approach literacy from the perspective of the "individual components of literacy", then these tests would be adequate measures of both initial skills and of progress. The larger question, however, continues to be "What are we trying to teach and why?" The "individual components of literacy" approach to teaching is at best limited and at worst self-defeating given its previous failure with adults with low levels of literacy. If the "functional competencies" or "portable skills" approaches are used, these instruments are inappropriate since they set a baseline and measure progress on the basis of skill applications unrelated to program goals. In this case, use of an academic-based assessment instrument would in all probability simply and unnecessarily reinforce the perception of failure of the adults taking the test.

If the state policymakers decide to approach literacy from the point of view of imparting basic functional competencies, then a different set of testing instruments is available. The GED test, the Adult Basic Learning Examination (ABLE) and the California Adult Student Assessment System (CASAS) test all are designed to measure skill in various areas of functional competence. This type of test or combinations of these tests can provide valuable evidence on the skill level and progress in particular functional areas. Programs have had difficulty, however, in designing a combination of assessment instruments that will adequately match the specific functional goals of the learner.[56] This is at least in part related to the broad differences in opinion about the specific functional competencies required to achieve particular goals.

If the approach is based on the concept of "portable skills," one particular assessment instrument stands out. That is the testing instrument used in the NAEP study. While there has been debate for some time among professional educators about the ability to teach a core set of skills that are transferrable, the NAEP study, through the use of its particular testing instrument, for the first time focused national attention on the portable skills approach to literacy education. Consequently, state policymakers are faced with a situation where a testing instrument exists; but program design for teaching portable skills is still in its infancy.

In addition to determining the skill level of learners, the use of initial diagnostic and assessment tests is also important to program managers in that they provide an overall picture of how well the program is progressing in meeting its goals. If very little progress is being made as demonstrated by the assessment tests, then the management should question its goals, its methods and/or its testing instruments.

While many programs purport to provide literacy education in the context of functional competencies, most programs measure initial skill levels through the use of standardized academic achievement tests. The TABE and the ABLE are the most widely used standardized tests, found in programs in all sectors. Of those programs using tests for functional competence, the Official GED Practice Test is widely used in all sectors. Interest or vocational inventories and learning style assessments are rare, despite the frequency with which educators mentioned tailoring instruction to student interests and learning style.[57]

Testing must be directly related to the question of "What are we trying to teach and why?" Programs must clearly define their instructional goals and choose a testing instrument that measures progress toward those goals. Programs that are designed to teach specific functional competencies such as those suggested in the APL study will probably have the most difficulty in finding tests to measure progress toward goals, simply because of the vast differences in the way programs define competencies. Programs focusing on the more traditional academic approach could probably use existing standardized tests more easily. For programs choosing to proceed with teaching generic problem-solving skills, an adaptation of the NAEP instrument from the Educational Testing Service is the only approach designed to date.

Considering the Motivation of the Learner

Even if programs are specifically tailored to target groups and the appropriate diagnostic and assessment instruments are used to determine the skill level of the learner, the motivation of the individual learner must also be considered.

Adult learning, as distinguished from childhood learning, is based on a perception of personal need.[58] If the individual is convinced that the ticket to economic independence is learning to speak English, and if economic independence is a valued commodity to the individual and in the community, then the learner will be motivated to participate in an English as a Second Language class, as long as he or she feels that the information is presented in such a way that the goal can be realized.

Thus we have two levels of motivation: One, motivating the individual to come to a class or program initially, and two, motivating that individual to remain in the program.

Motivation to Begin Instruction: An individual coming to an adult literacy improvement program comes with his or her own personal goals. While these individuals might fit within the target groups set by the governor to receive literacy enhancement for the broader purposes outlined by the governor, their own personal reasons for coming to the class may include other goals as well or may be entirely different. Unless some relationship between an individual's personal goals and motivations and the goals of the program is established, high dropout rates can be expected.[59]

The importance of addressing the goals and motivation of the learner in the context of overall policy goals of the program is underscored by David Harman. He suggests that "the role of the educator and the program designer, then, is not to impose an agenda, but rather to identify what participants want and what the particular situation requires."[60] The "particular situation" that Harman refers to could easily be defined as the broad policy objectives of the governor.

Motivation to Continue Instruction: Once in a program to upgrade their literacy skills, adult learners must feel that they are receiving assistance that moves them toward their particular goals. In an individual does not feel that the program is meeting his or her needs, he or she is quite likely to drop out.[61]

The literature on adult literacy suggests direction for state policymakers on this subject. One of Taggert's conclusions about the best approaches to literacy improvement is that "learning is accelerated and more directed when integrated with other activities and *pursued as a means to other ends*" (italics mine). [62] Case studies of literacy programs in different settings also support the position that greater advancements in literacy improvement are realized when "the substance of the program meshed with each participant's personal goals" and when "the program's literacy component was relegated to a secondary non-threatening position with which even the least literate in the group could cope."[63]

In both motivation to enroll and to continue instruction, the individual relates the content of instruction to the goal of instruction. Individuals are motivated to obtain certain goals: employment, employment advancement, ability to read to their children or to read a newspaper. They view literacy improvement as a means toward attaining these goals. If the content of instruction does not match the goal, then the individual will cease to participate. If the individual does not feel that adequate progress is being made, then he or she will be more inclined to drop out. High dropout rates for many literacy programs result from the mismatch of personal and program motives.[64] In too many cases, programs appear to fail to relate instruction to the goals and expectations – the motivation – of the individual participant.

Motivation is also related to the amount of time required to complete a task.[65] As noted earlier, improving literacy skills is an enormously time-consuming proposition. Gains are made slowly, although faster than through the elementary education system. In many cases, the slow progress is not sufficient to warrant the effort expended and adult students drop out. Mikulecky speculates that there is probably an 80 to 90 percent attrition rate for persons receiving less than one hundred hours of instruction.

The Setting for Adult Literacy Programs

Much discussion is available in the literature on adult literacy on the subject of the appropriate setting for literacy enhancement activities as well as on the relative effectiveness of certain methods of instruction. No conclusive evidence exists that suggests that workplace-based programs are more successful than, for example, community-based, school-based, or individual-based programs. Other factors, such as what is to be taught and targeting to the skill and need level of the learner, appear to be more important.

The issue of setting may well be more important to the program sponsor or administrator than to the learner. The sponsor will no doubt want to use its own delivery system to provide the service: private-for-profit sector programs provided on the workplace premises, ABE programs operated out of schools and community colleges, library programs using local libraries, and so on. Community-based program administrators will no doubt feel that location in a central facility in the neighborhood is essential. Volunteer-administered programs will base their programs where tutor and learner can conveniently meet.

To the learner, setting may only be important as it relates to proximity and access and as a symbol of the relationship of the program to the learner's personal goals. If the individual is motivated to upgrade his or her skills in order to obtain advancement within the company, then the setting within the worksite may be more convenient. Location in a secondary school or community service facility may make this learner feel out of place or emphasize feelings of inadequacy. Symbolically, program location at the workplace may underscore the relationship between his goals and the program. On the other hand, persons seeking to acquire pre-employment skills may feel perfectly at ease in a secondary school or community facility that is convenient and easily accessible.

For state policymakers, the most critical aspect of the program setting issue is its relationship to the convenience, skill level, goals, and motivation of the learner. No particular setting at first blush appears to be best. Rather, the setting of the program can be used as a tool to support and reinforce the learner.

Methods of Instruction

Discussion of methods of instruction usually includes a debate over whether, in teaching reading, the phonics-based method is superior to the sight-word or look-say method or the language experience method. As Harman points out, "fashion" changes in the accepted approach to teaching reading and other skills. "Indeed, the pendulum of reading instruction methods has been in constant motion for generations. It is likely to remain moving in perpetuity. It is also possible that the problem does not lie in the methods used for teaching, but rather in the neglect of a proper analysis of how, why, and what people learn."[66]

Much attention has been focused as well on the importance of computer-aided instruction. Computers were being used in most of the programs included in the NALP study and are being used as well in half of the programs operated in correctional institutions.[67]

Policymakers should beware of the temptation to move to the quick fix of computer-aided instruction. The computer as a tool for self-paced instruction is unquestionably valuable. Most students enjoy their encounters with computer-aided instruction, although many teachers resist its use. Computer-aided instruction is not the answer to the problem of adult literacy. It can, however, be a valuable added tool.

In using any computer-aided instruction, the first question that must be addressed continues to be "What is to be taught and why?" Most computer-aided instructional courses available today are simply adaptations of traditional academic materials. Thus, while apparent gains may come more quickly, the value of the skills learned in terms of their transferability and ability to be retained must be questioned in the same way as any other traditional academic approach to adult literacy. To the extent that computer-aided instructional materials can be developed to provide a broad range of experiences in which problem solving and information processing skills could be learned, their value would increase enormously.

In addition, computer-aided instructional materials must be used in the context of a well-formulated plan of addressing the skill levels, needs, and goals of the learner. Use of computers will not eliminate the need for staff sensitive to the needs of adult learners and the target group in particular.[68]

Any fruitful discussion of teaching methods must lead us back to the issue of what we are trying to teach and why. If a "century long debate of the perfect teaching method" [69] has not produced any conclusive decision, then perhaps, just perhaps, we are asking the wrong question. The fact is that people can and do learn to read using all sorts of methods. It may be that the key to their success lies in factors other than the specific instructional method used — factors such as motivation of the learner, a clear relationship between the personal goals of the learner and the goals of the program, a supportive learning environment, or a clear relationship of the subject matter being taught to its utility in other life situations.

Studies of adult literacy programs do provide some guidelines in considering the best approaches to instruction. Both the

NALP study and Ford Foundation funded reviews of adult literacy programs summarize the most successful approaches based on the perceptions of those working in the field.[70,71] These studies are reinforced by other experts in the field.[72,73] It is important to remember that these guidelines are drawn from summaries of anecdotal materials rather than from scientifically valid evaluations. These reviews emphasize the following observations:

- Learning depends on the applied or engaged learning time during instructional hours.
- Learning is enhanced when opportunities are supplied to apply skills in adult functional settings.
- The learning process becomes more feasible when flexibly scheduled and sequenced.
- Learning is more directed in the context of an instructional management system based on clear behavioral objectives.
- Learning is enhanced when administrators anticipate a multiplicity of learning goals and styles with a variety of program options.
- Learning may be accelerated when competency-based rather than time-based.
- Learning is enhanced when students are involved in decision making about their educational program.
- Learning is enhanced by positive reinforcement from instructional approaches and settings.
- Learning is easier for those who believe they can learn.
- Learning is nurtured by a structured and supportive environment which deals with personal problems.
- Learning is accelerated when caring teachers provide individual attention and assistance.

- Learning is enhanced by positive reinforcement from instructors.
- Learning is facilitated when a system of documenting student progress and achievement exists to give impetus and direction.

What is known about how the information should be conveyed in improving adult literacy skills?

To summarize, first, the skill level of the learner should be properly assessed in the context of a clear statement of what is to be taught and why. Assessment instruments must be carefully chosen to provide a baseline measure and an indication of progress in accord with the goals of the program.

Second, a clear relationship must be shown between the goals of the program and the goals of the individual learner. Ideally, the program goals would be viewed by the learner as instrumental to achieving a personal goal.

Finally, we know that more attention should be focused on the environment for learning, the motivation and goals of the learner, the specific learning needs of the learner, and the perceived relevance of the content of instruction to the learner than on the debate over the efficacy of a particular method of instruction.

WHO SHOULD CONVEY THE INFORMATION?

Even if a state's policy focused on the portable skills approach to adult literacy, clearly identified the broader policy goals for which improved literacy skills are necessary, identified and tailored its programs to specific target groups, and carefully matched its program to the skill levels and goals of the learners, it could still fail if the instructors were not properly prepared for the task nor familiar with the culture and values of the learners. In the context of considering who should convey the information to the adult learner, two different aspects of the issue should be explored. First is the level of education or training that should be required; second is the relationship between the racial/ethnic match of the learner and the instructor.

Education and Training of Instructors

The range of experience and skills among literacy instructors may exceed the range of skill levels among program participants. David Harman has observed that "In adult literacy programs, the range of qualifications of the instructors currently is very wide. Some have received a certain amount of training and are certified. Some have been trained and certified as school teachers and apply teaching skills that are inappropriate. Others have no training at all and are not properly equipped for the role."[74]

While the training prerequisites vary greatly from program to program, some generalizations can be made. In most Adult Basic Education Programs, the criteria used are in most cases those required for teacher certification in the state. At the other end of the credentialing scale are the volunteer tutoring programs where criteria usually include minimum educational attainment and a commitment to stay with the program.[75] In the middle of the scale are the community-based programs which "tend to be more academically flexible than in an ABE program, and more rigorous than in a volunteer tutor program".[76] There has been considerable debate in the past about the necessity of training for literacy instructors. Many people have clung with great tenacity to the assumption that "if you can read, you can teach someone to read." This assumption formed the basis of many volunteer administered tutoring programs. On this assumption policymakers often conclude that volunteers are a simple and cheap solution to solving the adult illiteracy problem. The solution is not that simple.

While volunteer tutors are a very valuable component of literacy improvement efforts and though they represent an enormous resource, instructors or facilitators must address the important issues of "What?", "Why?", "Who?", "How?", and "How Well?" If they are not trained to do so, they will surely experience high levels of failure in their efforts.[77]   In a monograph on the role of volunteers in combating adult illiteracy, the Business Council for Effective Literacy argues that "volunteers must be properly recruited and trained and the trainers of volunteers must themselves be trained. Moreover, volunteers must be supervised and supported by . . . experts and other professional personnel as needed. They must also be supplied with the instructional and other materials needed to function in their roles as tutors and staff. And, their performances must be evaluated."[78]

While no consensus exists on the level of education or training necessary for persons teaching adult literacy enhancement, an increasing number of people now believe that supervised teaching and in-service training are critical factors." [79, 80, 81] In the Ford Foundation report on adult literacy in the U.S., Harman states that "teachers require ongoing training to adjust their thinking and practice from a traditional (reading-as-decoding) model to one that truly connects learner-context-text-and-response."[82]

Adequate training for large numbers of instructors is not a realistic expectation, states Harman: "In the future as in the past, much of the work will be carried out by people who do not have adequate teaching skills and who, regardless of their good intentions, may be unequal to the task."   Instead, structured and intensive supervision should be provided for all staff, which would become, in effect, a form of in-service training, improving the skills of literacy instructors over time.[83]

B. Dalton Bookseller sponsored the development of "Guidelines for Effective Literacy Programs." These guidelines include a separate section on staff resources and state that "a literacy program should offer pre-service training to instructional and non-instructional staff that is suited to their skills and experience," and "should offer in-service training to instructors and other staff that continually improves their effectiveness in working with the program's adult learners."

Many community-based literacy programs use trained instructors or facilitators instead of untrained tutors. In a 1986 study of 31 community-based literacy programs, the Association for Community-Based Education found that "one key similarity is the use of trained instructors/group facilitators rather than (untrained) tutors." While the selection criteria vary greatly, most place considerable emphasis on pre-service and in-service follow-up, which typically consists of "an orientation session, a further de-briefing, and regular staff meeting at which instructors share problems and ideas."[84]

Similarly, the private sector is increasingly concerned about the training and supervision of those providing literacy education. The Business Council for Effective Literacy released in September of 1986 a Bulletin advising employers how they could develop an employee volunteer literacy program in their community. That bulletin pointed both to the needs for in-service training and supervision.[85]

Studies of adult literacy programs indicate that training of adult literacy instructors is now handled by the individual programs.[86,87] Consequently, program staff feel the need of help from others engaged in similar efforts. The experience of the New York City Adult Literacy Initiative provides a good case in point. In its 1986 report, staff development was identified as an important technical assistance need. The single most common technical assistance request related to staff development was for more networking.[88]

Staff of the program felt an enormous need for sharing their experiences with others with similar goals in order to acquire new approaches and techniques that may help them improve their performance and the performance of the learners.

Many existing adult literacy programs lack support in the area of staff development and training. Any state policy to improve literacy must focus on assuring that literacy instructors are adequately prepared at the program level to further the goals of the program. In the process of program design, state policymakers should pay attention to the resources necessary to train staff to provide literacy services. Since a serious effort to enhance literacy is likely to require a significant expansion of instructional services, the need to recruit and train instructors is an important factor in how far and how fast a state can move to address the problem.

Racial/Ethnic Mix of Learners and Instructors

Another consideration in designing a program that works is the importance of providing instructors that come from the same ethnic, racial or cultural background as the learners. Rainbow Research, Inc.'s., *Guidelines for Effective Adult Literacy Programs* states: "Adult learners could be more comfortable with the obvious presence of others of their ethnic group as instructors in the program, even if instructor-learner matches are made on other bases."[89] They further state that "a literacy program should continually strive to have the ethnic composition of the instructional staff reflect that of the learner population."

The ethnic/racial match of learners and instructors is important for reasons other than comfort. The 1979 Ford Foundation report on adult literacy notes that "respect for how learners see their world and what they can contribute as well as what they may wish to learn is an essential basis of education." [90] The report observes that

". . . (w)hen the (educational) encounter is between a dominant educational system and minorities whose history, traditions, and assumptions have been ignored and, often, denigrated," then a bridge of understanding must be found. Harman states that one way to fashion this bridge is to base literacy improvement in the context of the community from which the learners come. The employment of persons from the same community, culture, and values as the learners bridges this gap and shows, by example, that improvement of literacy skills is an attainable goal. For these reasons, many community-based programs use persons who have gone through the program as volunteers and assistants in helping others who come after them.[91, 92]

Mikulecky suggests that the real key to effective instruction is to find someone who can hold on to a learner for a long, long time. This quality obviously transcends racial and ethnic boundaries, although having a similar background and culture could clearly be a factor in one's ability to motivate a learner. Most adult learners have a family or work problems that must be dealt with if learning gains are to be made. An effective teacher/facilitator must be able to help the learner work through these problems, keep the individual's personal goal clear and help the individual make recognizable and sufficient progress toward that goal.

Although most experts in the field of adult literacy and most program operators and instructors stress having instructors/facilitators who are sensitive to the needs and goals of the learner and who appreciate and value the background and culture of the learner, one study suggests that these issues are subordinate rather than central. In 1975, Gordon Darkenwold hypothesized that adult minority students taught by minority teachers would make more gains in skill level than those taught by white teachers. His study showed that this was the case. However, when he looked further into the data he found that the minority teachers in most cases abandoned traditional teaching methods and adapted methods and materials that seemed to be more relevant to the learners. He also found that white teachers who followed these patterns showed greater gains with their students.[93] The results of this study underscore the importance of tailoring programs to the life circumstances, needs, goals and experiences of the learners. It reinforces the conclusion that traditional academic approaches to adult literacy education are not productive paths for policymakers to pursue.

In summary, we know that persons conveying information to adult learners or facilitating their learning process should be well trained in the philosophy, goals, and purposes of the program; provide assistance in nontraditional ways; continually receive supervision and in-service training to upgrade and improve their skills; and be well-versed in and respectful of the culture and community values of the learners.

HOW DO WE KNOW THAT THE SKILLS HAVE BEEN LEARNED?

The last and often most difficult question for state policymakers is the question of what has been accomplished. State policymakers will need to judge the efficacy of their policy and programs on two levels:

- To what extent are individual programs improving the literacy levels of their participants? and,
- Is the overall goal of the governor being met or is progress being made toward achievement of that goal?

The ability to answer these questions must be imbedded in the design of both policy and programs. This brings us full circle to the definition of literacy and back to the testing discussion about how one determines the skill level of learners. Both initial assessment and progress measures must be directly related to the question of "What are we trying to teach and why?" Progress or completion assessments must be made in order to determine whether or not programs and policies have in fact accomplished what they were designed to achieve.

It is important to keep in mind that evaluation is not simply a function of testing. Experience with adult literacy programs has shown that many individuals perform at higher levels on the job than they do in tests.[94] Policymakers must be aware of this in designing methods to determine the performance of particular programs or individuals.

To What Extent Are Individual Programs Improving the Literacy Levels of Participants?

In order to determine the extent to which literacy improvement programs are raising the literacy levels of participants, policymakers must return to the first question of program design: "What are we trying to teach and why?"   If the program's focus on who is to be taught is broad or unrelated to clear and measurable goals, if its methods of conveying the information are not designed to meet both the program goals and the needs of the learners, and if its instructors are not adequately prepared, then outcome-oriented evaluation will be difficult or impossible.

Evaluation procedures employed by existing adult literacy programs are in most cases not very sophisticated.[95] The NAPL study identified five barriers to effective program evaluation: 1) lack of time, 2) lack of training, 3) perceived lack of relevance, 4) difficulty in quantifying data, and 5) problems inherent in evaluating education for the educationally disadvantaged.[96]

In addition, program managers express vast differences of opinion on how to document progress as well as measure outcomes.[97]

When program managers discuss the inherent difficulties of evaluating educational outcomes for the "educationally disadvantaged," they may in fact be reflecting a wide disparity between the program's approach to literacy education and the learning needs of the adult student. That is, the goals, culture, and background of the students may be completely unrelated to the goals and instructional methods and materials used in the program and to the evaluation instruments used. To determine whether or not literacy programs are improving literacy levels of participants, individual programs must include in their design:

- the ability to assess routinely progress of participants; and,
- the ability to determine when the learner has acquired theneeded skills.

These assessments must be made in accordance with clearly stated program goals and a curriculum and instruction directly linked to achievement of those goals. The same considerations relating to the choice of an instrument for measuring the entry level skills of a learner apply here. The testing instrument should be selected for its direct relationship to the instructional goals of the program. Program outcomes also can be measured with more subjective evaluations, using testing as only one indicator of the educational progress of participants.

Program managers must know with certainty what they are expected to teach and why. Are they attempting to impart traditional skills through a compartmentalized, traditional academic approach? Are they trying to help learners develop functional competencies in several specific areas such as health and safety or employability? Are they attempting to expose learners to as many different life experiences as possible in order to develop a broad range of problem-solving skills, or are they attempting to help learners develop a set of portable skills that can be employed in any number of situations? Once the decision on program goals has been made, the tools used to evaluate progress as well as determine entry skills can be chosen accordingly, as was discussed at some length in Section IV of this chapter.

Follow-up of learners who have successfully completed the program is an important way to evaluate the effectiveness of a literacy program. This process enables a program to judge whether or not its assessment that an individual had acquired the requisite skills has any relationship to the achievement of the learner's personal goals and of the broader goals of the program. [98] Follow-up with persons who have dropped out of the program provides insight into why the program was not meeting the needs of those learners. Because programs experience such high dropout rates and have such great difficulty in helping individuals realize their personal goals, many programs have felt pressured to make misleading or downright dishonest claims in both their advertising and their reporting of success. [99] Follow-up data on why people drop out, such as the study done by Fitgerald, are essential to reorienting adult literacy efforts to improve literacy levels.

Program evaluation can also provide information on the effectiveness of individual program components and on the effectiveness of teachers.[100] Information in these two areas is important in order to determine corrective action. If a program has a clear statement of goals and a plan linking participation, the skill and need level of the learners, the motivation of the learner, the program settings and methods of instruction to overall goal achievement, then program managers will be able to reexamine each of these elements to more clearly identify opportunities for improvement.

As Harman and Hunter point out, programs cannot be evaluated in ". . .terms of political rhetoric or against the broad social reform they promise. The more important questions are whether program objectives are realistic, whether they are clearly communicated, and whether those who participate make visible and satisfying progress."[101]

To What Extent Are the Governor's Goals Being Met?

State policymakers should require the evaluation of adult literacy programs under state sponsorship or administrative review. They should also be able to translate the progress of individual programs into an overall assessment of progress toward realizing the state's policy goals. This kind of policy evaluation should reveal not only whether or not participants are receiving new skills but also whether the acquisition of those skills results in the desired policy outcome, such as getting a job, advancing in a job or better preparing preschool children.

For example, the governor may decide that the state goal is to improve literacy in order to increase employment. The program objective may be to move all unemployed persons to a functioning level of 300 on the NAEP scale in order to enable adults to get and keep jobs. State policymakers will want to be sure that programs are designed to increase levels of functioning in accordance with this definition and that the NAEP scale is employed as a means of testing and measuring progress. In addition, state policymakers will want to be sure that follow-up is provided at the program level to determine whether or not improved functioning on the NAEP scale does actually result in increased employment.

A governor could decide that he or she would focus on improving the employability skills of out-of-school unemployed youth. To be sure that progress was evaluated similarly across programs, the nature of the employability skills would have to be clearly specified and built into the programs. Guidelines for measuring progress would also have to be agreed upon prior to program implementation.

Unless evaluation is built into the original design of the governors policy and is included at every step in the translation into actual program, state policymakers will continue to find themselves in the situation they now face — one with no solid base of evaluative data on which to determine what works.

RESOURCE MANAGEMENT FOR IMPLEMENTATION

Policymakers can arrive at some important conclusions about what works or does not work and what direction they should proceed in developing policies and programs to enhance literacy. In summary, the following guidelines provide a framework for the development of state adult literacy policies for programs that stand a good chance of working:

• *Clearly specify what information, knowledge, or skills are to be imparted to adult learners and why it is important from a state policy perspective to assure the acquisition of those skills.* Regardless of the level of literacy on which a state chooses to focus its attention, the best evidence to date strongly suggests that imparting problem-solving and information-processing skills in a broad array of functional contexts that can be generalized is the best approach to program design. Although governors' offices may not want to involve themselves in what seem like specific program design details, it is important for them to ensure that operating programs and proposed programs meet the test of linking skills and policy outcomes.

• *Identify those groups of people who will require this type of intervention in order to meet the overall policy goals of the state.*

Identifying the populations to be targeted enables the policymaker to take into account the particular needs, problems, and life circumstances of the learner in approaching the task of improving literacy skills. Design specific methods of recruiting and retaining members of that group in literacy enhancement programs.

  • *Insure that program content is tailored to the skill and need levels of learners, considers the goals and motivations of individual learners, and provides a supportive environment for learning.* The skill level of the learner should be properly assessed in the context of a clear statement of what is to be taught and why. Assessment instruments must be chosen carefully to provide a baseline measure and an indication of progress in accord with the goals of the program. A clear relationship must be shown between the goals of the program and the goals of the individual learner. Also, an environment for learning must be established that will be convenient to the learner and will respect the culture and values of the learner.

  • *Assure that literacy instructors are adequately prepared to further the goals of the program.* Persons conveying information to adult learners or facilitating their learning process should be well trained in the philosophy, goals, and purposes of the program; trained in nontraditional and functional approaches to literacy education; continually receive supervision and in-service training to upgrade and improve their skills; and be well-versed in and respectful of the culture and community values of the learners.

  • *Build into the program design the ability to determine whether or not the requisite skills have been learned by the participants.* State policymakers will need to be able to judge the efficacy of their policies and programs both in terms of meeting the overall goals of the governor and in terms of improving the literacy levels of program participants.

144

At this point, state policymakers could be expected to ask where such programs exist that might be adapted for use in their state. The answer is that no one program has been identified as meeting all these criteria. Within the large number of of adult literacy programs in the nation, many good practices and principals can be identified. But many of the programs embodying some good practices violate other principals. Since there seem to be no clearly superior adult literacy programs that apply to all circumstances, state program designers must attempt to learn from the combined experience of practitioners and make their own choices.

State policymakers face two major choices:

- A mix-and-match approach of attempting to piece to-gether existing resources to fit into this framework and to approximate the policy goals of the state; or,
- A performance-based approach in which the governor sets forth the criteria for participation in state-sponsored programs and permits any of the existing provider organizations to bid.

The Mix-and-Match Approach to Literacy Program Implementation

One way of approaching the task of implementation is to identify in detail the full range of resources available. Some states have prepared needs and resources assessments as a first step to making a decision on resource allocation. The next and most difficult step in this approach is to analyze resources in terms of their conformity to the policy goals of the state and their adherence to a framework of policy guidelines such as the ones presented in this chapter. This is a difficult and time-consuming task, but one that must be accomplished in order to target resources to programs that have the greatest chance of success in achieving the governor's policy goals.

State staff would then have to make decisions about the extent to which each type of program, and perhaps each program, conformed to these policy goals and either negotiate for program changes or cease to fund them in favor of other alternatives. It is a job that would take years to complete and might not even be possible, due to the pressures likely to be mounted against tampering with individual programs. Staff could become bogged down in program detail, and the task of keeping the governor's goals and the policy framework clear and useful would become overwhelming.

A Performance-Based Approach to Literacy Program Implementation

Governors and their staffs must focus their attention on what *should* be provided in the way of literacy programs rather than what *is* being provided and how that differs from what is needed. Policymakers should place the burden on the programs to demonstrate that they are meeting the goals set forth by the governor, not the other way around.

In this approach, the governor would set the policy direction, identify the framework within which adult literacy programs would be supported, make the case to the public and use his or her office to further literacy enhancement efforts outside of state government. Any interested organization, firm, or individual would be free to compete for resources. The governor's policy would base resource allocation on performance in accordance with clearly stated objectives related to outcomes.

Performance-based systems are usually tried as add-ons to existing delivery systems and thus work best where additional financial resources are available. However, creating a two-tiered system is unnecessarily costly and doesn't make good use of the existing resources now being devoted to questionable outcomes. States interested in implementing a performance-based approach for all their programs will undoubtedly encounter some difficulties. First, the governor and staff will experience resistance from program managers anxious to maintain the *status quo* or to expand their own approach. The governor and staff must be completely committed to refocusing the approach of the existing system and must provide the time and attention necessary to insure that this takes place. Second, if the provider market is small, considerable work must be done to support its expansion. This might involve technical assistance and start-up funds. Finally, the governor and staff must be willing to withstand the pressure that will come from providers whose funds have been reduced or withheld for nonperformance.

A performance-based approach places the governor in the position of leadership rather than as arbitrator, permits immediate movement toward achieving the governor's goals and provides a clear standard and framework for progress rather than continued academic debate over the best ways of delivering services. It does not limit creativity and experimentation as it is outcome – rather than process – oriented. It also sets in place a requirement for program evaluation so that over time better information will be available for state policymaking.

Summary

State policymakers need to consider several critical issues as they design approaches to enhance the literacy of the population. This guide has focused on:

- The difficulty in defining the extent of the need for upgrading literacy skills and the limitations and utility of alternative definitions of literacy;

- The importance of addressing the problem of upgrading literacy skills in the context of the overall policy goals of the governor;
- The kinds of the targeting decisions the governor will face in narrowing the population to be addressed;
- The full range of powers and resources available to the state to address the problem;
- A framework within which to begin to craft programmatic solutions; and,
- An approach to implementation which will allow immediate movement and will build on the broad range of resources now available.

These issues require considerable analysis on the part of state policy staff to frame alternatives for the governor's decision. The final set of issues to be considered are those related to the role of the governor himself or herself in furthering the development and implementation of state action to improve literacy in the adult population.

Chapter 5 Notes

1. T. G. Sticht, et. al., *HumRRO's Literacy Research for the U.S. Army: Progress and Prospects* (Alexandria, Va.: HumRRO's Professional Paper 2-73, January, 1973).

2. Renee S. Lerche, Ed.,D., *Effective Adult Literacy Programs, A Pratitioner's Guide* (New York: The Cambridge Book Company, 1985), 171.

3. Anne Skagen, Editor, *Workplace Literacy* (New York: American Management Association, 1986), 24.

4. Richard L. Venezky, et. al., *The Subtle Danger, Reflections on the Literacy Abilities of America's Young Adults* (Princeton, New Jersey: Educational Testing Service, 1987), 7 - 8.

5. Carman St. John Hunter and David Harman, *Adult Illiteracy in the United States, A Report to the Ford Foundation* (New York: McGraw-Hill Book Company, 1985), 7, 57 - 59.

6. Renee S. Lerche, Ed.,D., *Effective Adult Literacy Programs, A Pratitioner's Guide* (New York: The Cambridge Book Company, 1985), 40.

7. Irwin S. Kirsch and Ann Jungeblut, *Literacy: Profiles of America's Young Adults* (Princeton, New Jersey: Educational Testing Service, 1986), 6.

8. David Harman, *Turning Literacy Around: An Agenda for National Action* (New York: Business Council for Effective Literacy, 1985), 5-6.

9. T. G. Sticht, et. al., *HumRRO's Literacy Research for the U.S. Army: Progress and Prospects* (Alexandria, Va.: HumRRO's Professional Paper 2-73, January, 1973).

10. Carman St. John Hunter and David Harman, *Adult Illiteracy in the United States, A Report to the Ford Foundation* (New York: McGraw-Hill Book Company, 1985), 75.

11. T. G. Sticht, et. al., *HumRRO's Literacy Research for the U.S. Army: Progress and Prospects* (Alexandria, Va.: HumRRO's Professional Paper 2-73, January, 1973).

12. Robert H. Cahen, *Illliteracy as an Economic Development Issue, Report # HR-19* (Youngstown, Ohio: The Center for Urban Studies, Youngstown State University, 1986), 14.

13. Renee S. Lerche, Ed.,D., *Effective Adult Literacy Programs, A Pratitioner's Guide* (New York: The Cambridge Book Company, 1985), 115.

14. Adult Performance Level Project, *Adult Functional Competency: A Summary* (Austin, Texas: The Adult Performance Level Project, 1975).

15. Renee S. Lerche, Ed.,D., *Effective Adult Literacy Programs, A Pratitioner's Guide* (New York: The Cambridge Book Company, 1985), 116.

16. Taggart, Robert, *The Comprehensive Competencies Program: A New Way to Teach, A New Way to Learn* (Washington, D.C.: Remediation and Training Institute, 1985).

17. Renee S. Lerche, Ed.,D., *Effective Adult Literacy Programs, A Pratitioner's Guide* (New York: The Cambridge Book Company, 1985).

18. Renee S. Lerche, Ed.,D., *Effective Adult Literacy Programs, A Pratitioner's Guide* (New York: The Cambridge Book Company, 1985), 115.

19. Carman St. John Hunter and David Harman, *Adult Illiteracy in the United States, A Report to the Ford Foundation* (New York: McGraw-Hill Book Company, 1985), 105.

20. Larry Mikulecky, *Functional Writing in the Workplace*, in L Gentry (Ed.), *Research and Instruction in Practical Writing* (Los Alamitos, California: Southwest Regional Laboratory for Educational Research and Development, 1980).

21. Larry Mikulecky, phone conversation of May, 1987.

22. IBID.

23. IBID.

24. Richard L. Venezky, et. al., *The Subtle Danger, Reflections on the Literacy Abilities of America's Young Adults* (Princeton, New Jersey: Educational Testing Service, 1987) 6.

25. Irwin S. Kirsch and Ann Jungeblut, *Literacy: Profiles of America's Young Adults* (Princeton, New Jersey: Educational Testing Service, 1986), 63 – 67.

26. IBID, 4.

27. IBID.

28. Larry Mikulecky, phone conversation of May, 1987.

29. IBID.

30. Anne Skagen, Editor, *Workplace Literacy* (New York: American Management Association, 1986), 19-20.

31. IBID, 19.

32. Richard L. Venezky, et. al., *The Subtle Danger, Reflections on the Literacy Abilities of America's Young Adults* (Princeton, New Jersey: Educational Testing Service, 1987), 8.

33. IBID.

34. Irwin S. Kirsch and Ann Jungeblut, *Literacy: Profiles of America's Young Adults* (Princeton, New Jersey: Educational Testing Service, 1986).

35. IBID, 67.

36. IBID.

37. Richard L. Venezky, et. al., *The Subtle Danger, Reflections on the Literacy Abilities of America's Young Adults* (Princeton, New Jersey: Educational Testing Service, 1987).

38. Larry Mikulecky, phone conversation of May, 1987.
39. T. G. Sticht, et. al., *HumRRO's Literacy Research for the U.S. Army: Progress and Prospects* (Alexandria, Va.: HumRRO's Professional Paper 2-73, January, 1973).
40. Larry Mikulecky, phone conversation of May, 1987.
41. IBID.
42. IBID.
43. Carman St. John Hunter and David Harman, *Adult Illiteracy in the United States, A Report to the Ford Foundation* (New York: McGraw-Hill Book Company, 1985), 110.
44. Renee S. Lerche, Ed.,D., *Effective Adult Literacy Programs, A Pratitioner's Guide* (New York: The Cambridge Book Company, 1985), 57-65, 83-96.
45. IBID, 67.
46. IBID.
47. Renee S. Lerche, Ed.,D., *Effective Adult Literacy Programs, A Pratitioner's Guide* (New York: The Cambridge Book Company, 1985), 57-82.
48. IBID, 58-65.
49. Anne Skagen, Editor, *Workplace Literacy* (New York: American Management Association, 1986), 19-20.
50. Renee S. Lerche, Ed.,D., *Effective Adult Literacy Programs, A Pratitioner's Guide* (New York: The Cambridge Book Company, 1985), 67.
51. Anne Skagen, Editor, *Workplace Literacy* (New York: American Management Association, 1986), 64.
52. Renee S. Lerche, Ed.,D., *Effective Adult Literacy Programs, A Pratitioner's Guide* (New York: The Cambridge Book Company, 1985), 83.
53. Association for Community Based Education, *Adult Literacy: A Study of Community Based Literacy Programs* (Washington, D.C.: Association for Community Based Education, 1986), 56.
54. Renee S. Lerche, Ed.,D., *Effective Adult Literacy Programs, A Pratitioner's Guide* (New York: The Cambridge Book Company, 1985), 84.
55. IBID, 87.
56. Renee S. Lerche, Ed.,D., *Effective Adult Literacy Programs, A Pratitioner's Guide* (New York: The Cambridge Book Company, 1985), 83 - 98.
57. Ibid, 92.
58. David Harman in Anne Skagen, Editor, *Workplace Literacy* (New York: American Management Association, 1986), 64.
59. Association for Community Based Education, *Adult Literacy: A Study of Community Based Literacy Programs* (Washington, D.C.: Association for Community Based Education, 1986), 28 - 29, 64 - 66.

60. David Harman in Anne Skagen, Editor, *Workplace Literacy* (New York: American Management Association, 1986), 64.

61. Carman St. John Hunter and David Harman, *Adult Illiteracy in the United States, A Report to the Ford Foundation* (New York: McGraw-Hill Book Company, 1985), 58 - 90.

62. Robert Taggart, *The Comprehensive Competencies Program: A New Way to Teach, A New Way to Learn* (Washington, D.C.: Remediation and Training Institute, 1985), 2 - 6.

63. David Harman, *Illiteracy: A National Dilemma* (New York: The Cambridge Book Company, 1987), 75 - 90.

64. Larry Mikulecky, phone conversation of May, 1987.

65. IBID.

66. David Harman, *Illiteracy: A National Dilemna* (New York: The Cambridge Book Company, 1987), 62.

67. Renee S. Lerche, Ed.,D., *Effective Adult Literacy Programs, A Pratitioner's Guide* (New York: The Cambridge Book Company, 1985), 133.

68. IBID, 133 - 134.

69. David Harman, *Illiteracy: A National Dilemma* (New York: The Cambridge Book Company, 1987), 61.

70. Renee S. Lerche, Ed.,D., *Effective Adult Literacy Programs, A Pratitioner's Guide* (New York: The Cambridge Book Company, 1985).

71. Robert Taggart, *The Comprehensive Competencies Program: A New Way to Teach, A New Way to Learn* (Washington, D.C.: Remediation and Training Institute, 1985).

72. David Harman, *Illiteracy: A National Dilemna* (New York: The Cambridge Book Company, 1987).

73. Larry Mikulecky, phone conversation of May, 1987.

74. David Harman, *Turning Literacy Around: An Agenda for National Action* (New York: Business Council for Effective Literacy, 1985), 29.

75. Association for Community Based Education, *Adult Literacy: A Study of Community Based Literacy Programs* (Washington, D.C.: Association for Community Based Education, 1986), 45.

76. IBID.

77. David Harman, *Illiteracy: A National Dilemna* (New York: The Cambridge Book Company, 1987), 84.

78. David Harman, *Turning Literacy Around: An Agenda for National Action* (New York: Business Council for Effective Literacy, 1985), 33.

79. Renee S. Lerche, Ed.,D., *Effective Adult Literacy Programs, A Pratitioner's Guide* (New York: The Cambridge Book Company, 1985), 219 – 226.

80. David Harman, *Turning Literacy Around: An Agenda for National Action* (New York: Business Council for Effective Literacy, 1985), 25 - 29.

81. Association for Community Based Education, *Adult Literacy: A Study of Community Based Literacy Programs* (Washington, D.C.: Association for Community Based Education, 1986), 73.

82. Carman St. John Hunter and David Harman, *Adult Illiteracy in the United States, A Report to the Ford Foundation* (New York: McGraw-Hill Book Company, 1985), xv, preface to paperback edition.

83. David Harman, *Turning Literacy Around: An Agenda for National Action* (New York: Business Council for Effective Literacy, 1985), 29.

84. Association for Community Based Education, *Adult Literacy: A Study of Community Based Literacy Programs* (Washington, D.C.: Association for Community Based Education, 1986), 48.

85. Business Council for Effective Literacy, *BCEL BULLETIN, Issue No.1* (New York: Business Council for Effective Literacy, September, 1986),8.

86. Renee S. Lerche, Ed.,D., *Effective Adult Literacy Programs, A Pratitioner's Guide* (New York: The Cambridge Book Company, 1985), 219 – 226.

87. Association for Community Based Education, *Adult Literacy: A Study of Community Based Literacy Programs* (Washington, D.C.: Association for Community Based Education, 1986), 48.

88. Literacy Assistance Center, Inc., New York City Adult Literacy Initiative, Final Report for Fiscal Year 1985 (New York: Literacy Assistance Center, 1985), 39.

89. Steven E. Mayer, Rainbow Research, *Guidelines for Effective Adult Literacy Programs* (Minneapolis: B. Dalton Bookseller, National Literacy Initiative, 1985), 3-1.

90. Renee S. Lerche, Ed.,D., *Effective Adult Literacy Programs, A Pratitioner's Guide* (New York: The Cambridge Book Company, 1985), 167 – 169.

91. Association for Community Based Education, *Adult Literacy: A Study of Community Based Literacy Programs* (Washington, D.C.: Association for Community Based Education, 1986), 47, 54.

92. Renee S. Lerche, Ed.,D., *Effective Adult Literacy Programs, A Pratitioner's Guide* (New York: The Cambridge Book Company, 1985).

93. Gordon Darkenwold, "Effective Approaches to Teaching Basic Skills to Adults", in *Sociology and Education*, (Volume 48, 1986).

94. Karl Kaigler, phone converstation, May, 1987.

95. Renee S. Lerche, Ed.,D., *Effective Adult Literacy Programs, A Pratitioner's Guide* (New York: The Cambridge Book Company, 1985), 171.

96. IBID, 173.

97. IBID, 171.

98. Renee S. Lerche, Ed.,D., *Effective Adult Literacy Programs, A Pratitioner's Guide* (New York: The Cambridge Book Company, 1985), 167 – 169.

99. Larry Mikulecky, phone conversation of May, 1987.

100. Renee S. Lerche, Ed.,D., *Effective Adult Literacy Programs, A Pratitioner's Guide* (New York: The Cambridge Book Company, 1985), 172.

101. Carman St. John Hunter and David Harman, *Adult Illiteracy in the United States, A Report to the Ford Foundation* (New York: McGraw-Hill Book Company, 1985), 58.

CHAPTER SIX

THE GOVERNOR'S ROLE IN ENHANCING ADULT LITERACY

INTRODUCTION

State government is not run like a corporation. Executive power is often diffuse; legislative effort is difficult to muster; the bureaucracy is hard to move. Moreover, the chief executive — the governor — often has little or no direct control over major systems of state government, especially the elementary and secondary education and the higher education systems. Since so many of the policies that need to be influenced in order to address the issue of adult literacy are not under the direct control of the chief executive, governor's staffs will want to consider carefully not only the role of the state in enhancing literacy but also the specific role of the governor and the executive branch.

The lack of direct control over the major state government systems that must be utilized to enhance adult literacy is one reason why so many governors have proposed commissions and coalitions as first steps in addressing the problem. Not only are state governments inherently limited in their ability to influence the behavior and commitment of citizens, but the governor may face substantial limits on his or her own power to move the systems that currently deal with the problems of adult literacy. Adult education programs may be governed by independent boards of education or separately elected chief state school officers. State higher education institutions may be separately governed and may resist attempts to cast them in a role of providing remedial education. Rooted in communities, often financed locally and responsive to local needs, community colleges may not see their role as one of enhancing literacy. Similarly, vocational education systems, with strong community ties and a desire to become involved in more technical education, may not be readily influenced by the governor's desire to enlist them in literacy efforts.

In most policy areas, the limits of the governor's influence can be stretched by exerting budget power, influence with the legislature, and public leadership. Adult literacy is no exception. The fact is, however, that many state government systems are governed by others or have traditional roles other than literacy enhancement. This complicates the governor's effort to develop strategies in this area and makes designing policy strategies a more delicate matter than most.

What then, is the most appropriate and effective role for the governor in addressing the issue of adult literacy? The answer to this question will, of course, vary from state to state, depending on the powers of the governor; his or her interest in spending time, effort, and political capital on the issue; and the extent to which other state officials are cooperative. Several roles suggest themselves:

LEADERSHIP

Under the rubric of leadership, the governor can play an important role in mobilizing public opinion, directing both public and private resources to the problem, and clarifying the nature and extent of the problem. The governor can also publicly link the issue of adult literacy with other important goals such as jobs and productivity. The governor can propose major government and private sector initiatives to enhance literacy in the context of these goals.

The governor can raise public awareness of the issue of adult literacy and help to define its extent. Together with volunteer groups, the media, businesses, and others, governors individually and collectively as the National Governors' Association have called attention to the literacy issue and have begun efforts to increase public awareness of the problem. Governors have formed literacy coalitions, worked with the media to promote utilization of literacy services, exhorted businesses to help, and sponsored outreach campaigns.

Because the problem of adult literacy is so large and complex, governors will have to sustain this kind of public awareness effort and direct it toward more specific actions to combat illiteracy or enhance literacy. As generalized concern over literacy coalesces in the public mind into demands for action, governors and other state policymakers will have to be ready to advocate specific initiatives to be taken by government, the private sector, and individuals. In addition, the focus of attention on literacy will have to be sustained through several years of effort, much as the education reform movement has seen succeeding "waves" of attention, proposals, legislation, and implementation efforts.

The governor can call together other leaders in the state, from local government, business, labor, and academia and influence their responses to the issue. Governors are very effective as conveners. Govenor's offices have sponsored conferences and coalitions to address the issue of adult literacy. They have brought together leading representatives of education, business, labor, and local governments to assess the problem and recommend solutions.

Governors can do more to bring people and institutions that are not usually concerned with literacy into the literacy movement. They can ask health care providers, for example, to consider building literacy assessment and services into their system. They can bring businesses together with educational institutions and community-based service providers to discuss how they can cooperate to address the literacy problem. Governors can also convene local government leaders to enlist them in the literacy effort.

The governor can focus the efforts of state government and the private sector on literacy enhancement policies that will help achieve other goals, such as economic development, productivity, or educational improvement. Governors often help the public reach policy conclusions that are not otherwise readily apparent. They have been very successful in stressing the close connection between elementary and secondary education and jobs. Since the literacy of the workforce affect the entire economic system of a state, this connection can be reinforced for employers, governments and others. Governors can address disparate interest groups, each with their own agendas, and ask them to consider how their agendas might be adjusted to contribute to literacy efforts. Day care providers and university faculty, for example, do not usually think of themselves as potential sources of literacy assistance for parents. With the governor's leadership, these groups and others can begin to examine their own systems to determine how they might fit into a governor's literacy initiative.

Similarly, governors can exert leadership within state government to ask operating agencies who usually would not consider themselves responsible for adult literacy to adjust policies in order to enhance literacy. Economic development agencies, for example, have begun to respond to gubernatorial demands that they expand their visions of economic development to include labor force development. Community development agencies are working with local governments not only on downtown renewal or housing, but also on issues such as education and literacy.

Governors can extend the concern with adult literacy to virtually every agency in state government and deeply into the operations of school districts, local governments, and others who receive state funds or are regulated by the state. As Chapter 3 indicated, there are significant policy opportunities in functional areas such as transportation, community development, business regulation, and taxation that will not be considered unless the governor makes it clear that all the tools and powers of state government are available for the effort to enhance literacy.

The governor can coordinate efforts within state government and elsewhere. Another level of gubernatorial leadership involves demanding that policies and programs to address adult literacy be accomplished in a coordinated fashion. Demanding that separate agencies and interest groups work together, fashioning interdepartmental policies, and packaging resources from disparate sources are all functions that governors' offices can and do perform every day. With much of the governance of programs addressing adult literacy removed from the governor's direct control, this function will be more difficult to perform with adult literacy policy, but gubernatorial leadership can make coordination happen.

When allocating resources or deciding whether to support legislation, the governor can insist that literacy policies and programs be targeted to the most important groups. Governors can also demand that state officials coordinate literacy policies with those outside of state government who are already shouldering much of the burden of providing literacy services and raising public awareness. Since state government has a tendency to become insular and develop policy in a vacuum unless pushed by the governor, this is an important leadership role for the governor.

By itself, coordination is a meaningless goal. If governors demand the coordination of programs in order to produce measurable results, however, the fragmentation in program operations that now seems to exist can be overcome. Structuring the coordinating mechanisms of state government so that they focus on measurable outcomes will be an important role for the governor's staff.

Gubernatorial leadership always involves setting priorities. Since most governors will not choose adult literacy as the highest priority issue—compared, for example, to economic development, education reform, welfare reform, fighting drugs, or tax reform, literacy policy must be developed in the context of gubernatorial leadership on these other issues. Strong evidence exists that approaches to all these issues can be enhanced by attention to the literacy issue. As a result, governors can exert leadership on the adult literacy issue even as they pursue other high priority goals.

RESOURCE ALLOCATION

The governor shares with the legislature the power to allocate state resources. The budget-making power of the governor is perhaps his most important role. Even in periods of fiscal restraint, the governor normally has the ability to shift resources within the budget and can make decisions about allocating revenue growth. The budget process focuses policymaking and demands disciplined decisions about priorities.

In this context, the governor can not only expand resources for literacy services, he can also use the budget to influence parts of state government he does not control to join in efforts to enhance literacy. The governor can use the budget process to stimulate creative thinking about approaches to literacy, engender specific program proposals, and demand targeted and coordinated services. Governors can utilize the budget process and their power to allocate resources in a number of ways:

Designating Adult Literacy as a High Priority in the Budget Process. Governors can signal that adult literacy is a high priority, connected closely to high priority goals of the administration. They can let it be known, formally or informally, that agency budget requests for funds to address literacy will receive close scrutiny and possible allocation of funds. In some states, governors issue budget guidelines that formally identify high priority programs, where agencies can expect that well thought out proposals will receive support. In others, the governor may assign planning staff and budgeting staff to stimulate budget proposals and to insist that they be targeted to the governor's priorities and contain evaluation and outcome measurement components.

Assigning Staff to Develop a Comprehensive Initiative or Package. Another approach is to assign planning and budgeting staff to develop a set of budget and policy options that enable the governor to advocate an adult literacy initiative or package in the budget itself, the State of the State Message, and the Budget Message. Although many governors have created literacy coalitions and have stimulated policy development efforts in state government, few have advocated full-fledged initiatives or packages designed to address the issue of literacy. Working with state coalitions and using the budget and planning processes within the state, governor's offices are likely to be in the midst of developing adult literacy initiatives right now. The governor's role is to set the priorities within the budget and to judge whether or not policy options presented to him by agencies and his own staff are sufficiently compelling to include in the budget.

Using the High Priority of Adult Literacy Enhancement as a Condition for Support of other Budget Actions. Governors can also use budget-making power to inject the consideration of adult literacy issues into policy debates within the elementary and secondary education budget, the human services budget, the natural resources budget, the higher education budget, and elsewhere. The governor may, for example, partially condition his support for budget expansions for community colleges or higher education institutions on cooperation in providing remedial education services to a certain target group. This use of the budget process can occur not only during budget preparation but also within the legislature as budgets are changed and ratified. Some governors, for example, have conditioned their support for various "workfare" proposals on the provision of adequate adult basic education funds as well as funds for child care and health care. This kind of "horse trading" cannot be effective, however, if the policy staff and the governor do not have a clear idea of exactly what adult literacy enhancement efforts they need to promote and the outcomes they want to achieve.

Using the Budget Process to Reallocate Resources within Existing Programs and Encourage Accountability and Performance Measurement. Governors and their budget staffs can also use the budget process to ask serious questions about current literacy efforts funded by state government. They can demand that programs currently providing literacy services be more accountable and report outcome measures. They can use the budget process to suggest reallocations, targeting resources to those adults whose literacy skills are most critical and coordinating resources across agency lines. The budget process can also be used to encourage or require existing programs to report on the outcomes of their programs and to evaluate the methods by which literacy services are provided. In addition, agencies can be encouraged to build new incentives for performance into the funding mechanisms for existing programs. Adult vocational education funds flowing to community colleges or private providers, for example, could be tied to achievement of skill levels, job placement, or the income performance of graduates. The budget process is a mechanism through which agencies can be induced to think seriously about injecting performance measures and new incentives into their everyday operations.

Through the resource allocation process, the governor can reform existing programs, redirect resources to high priority target groups, and engender new approaches to enhancing literacy. The budget can become an important tool in linking adult literacy policies with gubernatorial priorities.

INSTITUTIONAL CHANGE

One of the complexities of developing policies for adult literacy is that no single institution or system has the primary responsibility for meeting the literacy needs of the adult population. Higher education institutions view remediation as a necessary evil. Community colleges are oriented toward awarding associate degrees or providing technical education. Vocational education programs see basic literacy as a prerequisite for vocational training. Even the job training system tends to emphasize specific skills training rather than literacy or imparting more generalized literacy skills. Adult basic education programs have often been the stepchildren of the elementary and secondary education system. As a result, adult literacy efforts have received little institutional support and nurturing from the major political and economic forces in most states.

The governor can play an important long-term role in enhancing literacy by helping major insitutions to redefine their roles to include a major emphasis on the literacy of the adult population. Until recently, adult literacy policies have been perceived as something that states had to attend to because the school systems just did not function adequately. Many politicians and policymakers viewed adult literacy efforts as secondary to reforms in the education or training systems. If these systems could be made to work properly, the problem of literacy would go away.

As the discussion in Chapters One and Two revealed, the hope that the problem of adult literacy will resolve itself is a false one. Literacy definitions and needs will expand as the "receding horizon" effect takes hold. The rapidly changing economy will always require a large investment in literacy, lifelong education, training, and retraining. Recognizing this fact, governors can help to locate the responsibility for continuing attention to the literacy issue in institutions that will survive long after literacy coalitions have passed from the economic and political landscape.

Governors need to consider how to institutionalize literacy policy by placing the responsibility for adult literacy performance with institutions that will survive and adapt. Possibilities include expanding the role of the elementary and secondary education system, charging the community college system with responsibility for ensuring that adult literacy needs are met or creating new entities whose primary missions are to address this issue. In the intermediate term, the governor can create interagency mechanisms to help coordinate and direct the response of state governments, but in the long term a clearly defined institutional home for adult literacy policy must be sought.

Since creating new and self-perpetuating institutions or agencies is probably unfeasible and unwise, the governor will probably have to work with the legislature and other elected officials to inject the mission of ensuring adult literacy into one or more existing insitutional systems. Governors probably will not want to lodge this responsibility in their own offices. The track record of similar groups, such as governors' energy offices, or governors' offices on women or minorities, does not hold much promise for this approach to long-term institutional change.

The elementary and secondary education system now governs most of the programs involved in adult literacy enhancement, including adult basic education and vocational education. Charging the elementary and secondary education system with this responsibility or asking that system to emphasize adult literacy over other priorities may burden an already overburdened system. Current education reforms are straining the capacity of the elementary and secondary education system to respond. Adding the long-term responsibility for ensuring an adequately skilled adult population may not be feasible.

To lodge this responsbility with the community college system will require a change in the way most two-year colleges look at themselves and define their missions. Most community college systems have eschewed their roots in vocational and technical education and have attempted to become more like four-year institutions of higher learning. Governors may want to reevaluate this trend and determine whether a major charter for community colleges might be ensuring literate adults.

Regardless of where the institutional responsibilities for adult literacy policy may lie in the future, the governor can begin to seek changes in the public schools that will prevent high drop-out rates, changes in vocational and technical education institutions that will stress literacy and problem-solving skills, changes in job training priorities to emphasize literacy, and many other institutional reforms. Pressing for these types of institutional changes, governors may have the most long-term impact on the problem of adult literacy.

CHAPTER SEVEN

CONCLUSION

Governors have helped focus public attention on adult literacy. During the next few years, significant actions will have to accompany public commitment in dealing with adult literacy. In moving from goals to objectives and strategies, policymakers should carefully consider the five central issues discussed in previous chapters:

Defining and Measuring Literacy. Policymakers must recognize that literacy is a continuum of skills rather than an all-or-nothing state. As a basis for policy development, policymakers must estimate the numbers and characteristics of persons associated with identifiable ranges on the continuum. The extent to which definitions are important and measurements crucial will vary, depending on the link between specific target groups and the governor's overall goals.

Targeting the Analysis. The governor must consider how the current literacy level of the population affects other state policy goals, such as stimulating economic development, reducing dependency, and enhancing educational opportunities. Connecting gubernatorial goals to estimates of the size of the problem provides the basis for deciding which target groups on the literacy continuum should be addressed. Targeting permits policymakers to cast the issue in a more manageable form.

Considering the Full Range of Policy Tools Available to Address the Problem. To insure that policy strategies to enhance literacy are effective, the governor will have to employ all the relevant tools and powers at his command and will have to influence many more not under his direct control. These include: direct service provision; indirect service provision through purchase or funding; setting the conditions of benefits and employment; taxation and revenue collection; regulation and stimulation of private enterprise; licensing individuals; mandating local government responses; and leadership models.

Designing Programs that Work. Policymakers should use the following guidelines as a framework for the development of state adult literacy policies for effective programs:

- Clearly specify what information, knowledge, or "portable" skills are to be imparted to adult learners and why it is important from a state policy perspective to assure the acquisition of those skills;
- Identify, within the broad target groups identified by the governor, those persons who will require this type of intervention in order to meet the overall policy goals of the state;
- Insure that program content is tailored to the skill and need levels of learners, considers the goals and motivations of individual learners, and provides a supportive environment for learning;
- Assure that literacy instructors are adequately prepared to further the goals of the program;
- Build into the program design the ability to determine whether or not the requisite skills have been learned by the participants; and

- Implement programs through a performance-based approach wherein resources are available in accordance with clearly stated objective-related outcomes.

Clarifying the Governor's Role. State policy staff should be certain that strategies presented to the governor are consistent with the role he or she wishes to play and are realistic given the range of powers of the governor. The governor may approach the issue of literacy enhancement through exercise of his or her powers of leadership or resource allocation or through his or her ability to effect institutional change.

A comprehensive and effective policy for improving literacy will meet the following criteria:

- The policy identifies clearly broad gubernatorial goals to which the literacy initiative relates;
- Measurable outcome-oriented policy objectives relate to the achievement of gubernatorial goals;
- Specific strategies address accomplishment of these measurable objectives; and,
- Strategies are consistent with the governor's preferred role and are feasible given the resources available.

As an example, consider a selected list of target groups and the specific objectives identified by one state staff in preparing an adult literacy initiative for the governor. Strategies for implementation are still in the process of development:[1]

Goal	Target Group	Objective	Measure
Provide Economic Opportunity	Displaced Workers	Improve basic skills by 2 grade levels to enable workers to secure jobs at comparable wages	Comparable wage
Reduce Dependency	AFDC Mothers	Improve skills so that recipients are eligible for job training & day care	Entry into job training
Improve Education	Mothers with preschool children	Enhance reading skills of nonreading mothers by 2-3 grade levels	School readiness of kindergartners

Because the conditions in each state regarding adult literacy are unique, each state will have to develop its own policy goals, objectives, and strategies for enhancing adult literacy. Several approaches to developing adult literacy strategies are summarized:

Strategy 1: Political Leadership. Perhaps the most important leadership role for the governor is to continue to focus public attention on the adult literacy issue and on the need for skills enhancement to meet economic challenges. Governors can exert considerable influence to help change the popular notion that reading, writing, math, and communications are not very important. Governors collectively can urge public and private groups to help create a culture wherein literacy enhancement is expected and valued. The governor's office can coordinate state agency efforts in dealing with the adult literacy issue. Another way in which the governor can coordinate the governmental response is by becoming a model employer, changing state personnel and training priorities to stress adult literacy, and providing workplace literacy training. States can also work with local governments in providing workplace literacy programs and in offering basic skills training programs to potential employees.

Perhaps the most significant step a governor can take *vis a vis* the private sector is to encourage firms to develop the institutional capacity to respond to the need for enhanced literacy skills. Governors can help business leaders develop a conscious attention to the training needs of their employees.[2] In order to be credible in asking the public to respond to the problems of adult literacy, governors will have to propose specific and substantive ways in which the public can attack the problem. Governors will have to show volunteers how they can best fit into the overall state adult literacy strategy. This strategy must recognize that while volunteers can be a significant resource in improving literacy skills in certain target groups, they cannot be the central focus of a successful strategy. When governors take steps to stimulate volunteer efforts, state officials should assure that they, private sector firms, and other providers furnish the support that is needed to train and use volunteers most effectively.

Strategy 2: Refocus Governmentally Financed Programs. Refocusing and reallocating resources within existing appropriations for literacy service programs should be considered a major policy strategy to enhance adult literacy. Making full use of the program resources available to the state is an essential and central element of an overall strategy to enhance literacy. In order to assure that the governor's goals and objectives are being met, each program that provides adult literacy services either directly by the state or indirectly through the community should operate in accordance with the broad guidelines outlined in Chapter 5.

Strategy 3: Create New Service Programs to Enhance Adult Literacy. All state resources combined probably reach less than 5 percent of the population needing assistance, even assuming optimistic estimates of the size of the potential target population. States must be prepared to commit additional resources to address this problem. In developing proposals for service expansion, state leaders should adopt a performance-based approach which ties financing of literacy services to measurable literacy improvements among individuals in specific target groups.

One way to expand literacy services and at the same time target resources would be to provide literacy service vouchers or certificates to specific target groups. Under this approach, the certificates would be worth money to private or public sector providers who could establish that the bearer of the certificate had received a certain level of literacy training. Ideally, a certificate program would pay the provider only when a degree of student progress had been achieved. State leaders considering service expansions are attempting to package proposals for new and expanded programs into performance-based strategies that are focused on specific target groups, rely on a variety of delivery mechanisms, and are designed to be accountable to the governor and legislature.

Strategy 4: Use Other State and Local Powers to Enhance Literacy. The extent of the problem is so large that a strategy relying solely on the provision of new government programs would require efforts equal to the creation of an entire new elementary and secondary education system or another system of higher education. Since no state budget will accommodate this kind of commitment, state leaders will have to use other powers and provide incentives to the private and not-for-profit sectors of the economy in order to stimulate the provision of literacy services. Policy options using the regulatory, tax, and licensing systems may become attractive to governors seeking to induce the private sector and others to address the issue. Alternatively, receipt of certain social service benefits could be conditioned on enrollment in literacy improvement programs. Options such as these are not without disadvantages. Each raises serious social policy questions that must be fully and carefully debated in order to balance issues of equity and access with the goal of literacy improvement.

Strategy 5: Influence Major Public Institutions to Take Responsibility for Literacy Enhancement. Another strategy involves using the office of the governor to influence the operation of other public institutions over which the governor has no direct control. The most recent example of this approach is in the area of reform of the elementary and secondary education system. Across the country, governors exerted leadership with the public and with their legislatures to change education policy, even in states where there were separately elected chief state school officers and boards of education. This same approach could be used as well in the area of adult literacy which has traditionally fallen into the purview of the education system. The momentum formed by many successful education reform initiatives could be used to further the cause of adult literacy.

Most of the nation's governors are developing adult literacy initiatives based on some of the policy strategies outlined above. With the help of the Council of State Policy and Planning Agencies, ten state staffs have worked together to develop specific goals, objectives, and strategies for enhancing literacy. These strategies range from very specifically targeted programs to broad commitments to ensure that everyone in a single state has a high school education or its equivalent. State governments are poised to take significant actions to address the issue of adult literacy in America. With a clear vision of both the problems and opportunities posed by the literacy issue, governors and other state leaders can make literacy a major priority for the nation's future.

Chapter 7 Notes

1. State Team proposal at Academy 1, Kansas City, June, 1987.
2. Tony Carnevale, Opening Remarks, Adult Literacy Academy, Kansas City, June, 1987.

BIBLIOGRAPHY

Adult Performance Level Project. *Adult Functional Competency: A Summary* (Austin, Texas: University of Texas at Austin, 1975).

Adult Performance Level Project. *Final Report: The Adult Performance Level Study* (Austin, Texas: University of Texas at Austin, 1977).

American Bar Association. *Lawyers for Literacy, A Bar Leadership Manual* (Washington, D.C.: American Bar Association, Task Force on Literacy, 1987).

Applebee, Arthur, Judith Langer, and Ina Mullis. *Learning to Be Literate in America* (Princeton, N.J.: Educational Testing Service, 1986).

Arizona Joint Task Force on Adult Illiteracy. *Unlocking the Future: Adult Literacy in Arizona* (Phoenix: Governor and Superintendent's Joint Task Force on Adult Illiteracy, 1986).

Ashcroft, Governor John. *Governors' Bulletin* (Washington, D.C.: National Governors' Association, April, 1987).

Association for Community Based Education. *Adult Literacy: A Study of Community Based Literacy Programs* (Washington, D.C.: Association for Community Based Education, 1986).

Business Council on Effective Literacy. "Developing An Employee Volunteer Literacy Program" (*BCEL Bulletin*, September, 1986).

Butler, Erik and Andrew Hahn. "The Literacy-Employment Equation: Education for Tomorrow's Jobs" (San Francisco: Far West Laboratory for Educational Research and Development, 1985).

Cahen, Robert. "Illiteracy as an Economic Development Issue" (Youngstown, Ohio: The Center for Urban Studies, Youngstown State University, 1986).

Chute, Adrienne. "Meeting the Literacy Challenge" (Washington, D.C: U.S. Department of Education, Office of Educational Research and Improvement, Library Programs, March, 1987).

Conklin, Nancy F. and Janise Hurtig. *Making the Connection: A Report for Literacy Volunteers Working with Out-of-School Youth* (Portland Oregon: Northwest Regional Educational Laboratory, 1986).

Corporate Roles in Public Education Project. *Basic Skills in the U.S. Work Force* (Center for Public Resources, 1983).

Darkenwold, Gordon. "Effective Approaches to Teaching Basic Skills to Adults" in *Sociology and Education* (Volume 48, 1986).

Drucker, Peter. *Management* (London: Pan Books, 1979).

Duggan, Paula. *Literacy at Work, Developing Adult Basic Skills for Employment* (Washington, D.C.: Northeast-Midwest Institute, the Center for Regional Policy, 1985).

Employment and Training Administration. *Illiteracy in America: Background Notes* (Washington, D.C.: July, 1986, unpublished).

Fingeret, Arlene. "Adult Literacy Education: Current and Future Directions" (Columbus, Ohio: The National Center for Research in Vocational Education, 1984).

Harman, David. *Illiteracy: A National Dilemna* (New York: The Cambridge Book Company, 1987).

Harman, David. *Turning Literacy Around: An Agenda for National Action* (New York: Business Council for Effective Literacy, 1985).

Hull, William, Ernest Fields, and Judith Sechler. *Industrial Literacy Programs: Final Project Report* (Columbus, Ohio: The National Center for Research in Vocational Education, 1986).

Hunter, Carman St. John and David Harman. *Adult Illiteracy in the United States* (New York: McGraw Hill, 1985).

Insight. "Curse It, Count It, Cure It: The Arithmetic of Illiteracy" (*Insight*, Sept. 29, 1986).

Irwin, Paul M. "Adult Literacy Issues, Programs and Options" (Washington,D.C.: Congressional Research Service, October 20, 1986).

Kangisser, Dianne. *Pioneers and New Frontiers: The Role of Volunteers in Combating Adult Illiteracy* (New York: Business Council for Effective Literacy, 1985).

Kirsch, Irwin and Ann Jungeblut. *Literacy: Profiles of America's Young Adults* (Princeton, N.J.: Educational Testing Service, 1986).

Kozol, Jonathan. *Illiterate America* (New York: Anchor Press/ Doubleday, 1985).

Lerche, Rene (ed.). *Effective Adult Literacy Programs: A Practitioners Guide* (New York: Cambridge, 1985).

Literacy Assistance Center. "New York City Adult Literacy Initiative: Final Report for Fiscal Year 1985" (New York: Literacy Assistance Center, 1986).

Mayer, Steven. Guidelines for Effective Adult Literacy Programs (Minneapolis: B. Dalton Bookseller National Literacy Initiative, 1985).

McMichael, Kathryn L. "An Overview of the Adult Literacy Initiative in America" (Washington D.C.: National Commission for Employment Policy, 1987).

Mikulecky, Larry. "Functional Writing in the Workplace", in L Gentry (Ed.), *Research and Instruction in Practical Writing* (Los Alamitos, California: Southwest Regional Laboratory for Educational Research and Development, 1980).

National Association of State Boards of Education. "State Adult Literacy Initiative: Report of a National Conference and Survey of State Programs" (December, 1986).

National Diffusion Network. "Adult Literacy: Programs That Work" (Washington, D.C.: U.S. Department of Education, 1984).

Office of Deputy Under Secretary for Planning, Budget and Evaluation. "Adult Illiteracy Estimates for States" (Washington, D.C.: U.S. Department of Education, 1986).

Office of Strategic Planning and Policy Development. "Illiteracy in America: Background Notes" (Washington, D.C.: Employment and Training Administration, U.S. Department of Labor, 1986).

Office of Vocational and Adult Education, "Job Training Partnership Act Planning Guide for Adult Education State Directors" (Washington, D.C.: U.S. Department of Education, no date).

Perelman, Lewis. *Technology and Transformation of Schools, Public Education Strategies for a More Competitive Nation* (Washington, D.C.: National School Boards' Association, March, 1987).

Rush, R. Timothy, Alden J. Moe, and Rebecca L Storlie. *Occupational Literacy Education* (Newark, Delaware: International Reading Association, 1986).

Secretary of Labor's Task Force on Economic Adjustment and Worker Dislocation. *Economic Adjustment and Worker Dislocation in a Competitive Society* (Washington, D.C.: U.S. Department of Labor, 1986).

Semerad, Roger. "Remarks at Workforce 2000 Briefing" (Nashville, Tennessee, October, 1986).

Skagen, Anne, editor. *Workplace Literacy* (New York: American Management Association, 1986).

Stedman, James B. *Education in America: Reports on its Condition, Recommendations for Change* (Washington, D.C.: Congressional Research Service, Education and Public Welfare Division, October, 1986).

Sticht, T.G., et. al. *HumRRO's Literacy Research for the U.S. Army: Progress and Prospects* (Alexandria, Virginia: HumRRO's Professional Paper 2-73, January, 1973).

Taggart, Robert. *The Comprehensive Competencies Program: A New Way to Teach, A New Way to Learn* (Washington, D.C.: Remediation and Training Institute, 1985).

The Commission on Higher Education and the Adult Learner. "Adult Learners and National Priorities: Emerging State and Federal Policies" (Proceedings of a Conference, November 1985).

The National Advisory Council on Adult Education. *Illiteracy in America: Extent, Causes and Suggested Solutions* (Washington, D.C.: The National Advisory Council on Adult Education, Literacy Committee, 1986).

U.S. Department of Commerce, Bureau of the Census. *State and Metropolitan Area Data Book* (Washington, D.C.: U.S. Government Printing Office, April 1986).

U.S. Department of Education. *Adult Literacy Estimates for the States* (Washington, D.C.: Office of Planning, Budget and Evaluation, 1986, unpublished).

U.S. Department of Labor. *Workforce 2000* (Washington, D.C.: U.S. Department of Labor, 1987).

Vaughan, Roger, Robert Pollard, and Barbara Dyer. *The Wealth of States* (Washington, D.C.: Council of State Policy and Planning Agencies, 1986).

Venszky, Richard L., Carl F. Kaestle, and Andrew M. Sum. *The Subtle Danger: Reflections on the Literacy Abilities of America's Young Adults* (Princeton, N.J.: Center for the Assessment of Educational Progress, Educational Testing Service, 1987).

Waller, Patricia and Robert Hall. "The Extent and Distribution of Functional Illiteracy in North Carolina as Determined by the Use of the Oral Driver License Examination" (Chapel Hill, N.C.: University of North Carolina Highway Safety Research Center, 1976).

Washington Post. "The New Cutting Edge In Factories: Education" (*Washington Post*, April 14, 1987).

OTHER CSPA WORKS OF INTEREST:

Creating Opportunity: Reducing Poverty Through Economic Development, by Hugh O'Neill, CSPA, 1985. A ground-breaking analysis of the ways economic opportunity can be provided for "the working poor, the welfare poor, the elderly poor and the 'underclass'," the book presents a strategy to achieve that end. $16.95.

The Game Plan: Governance with Foresight, John Olsen and Douglas Edie, CSPA, 1982. An introduction to strategic planning concepts and practical advice on their application to public policy decisionmaking. $16.95.

Thinking Strategically: A Primer for Public Leaders, Susan Walter and Pat Choate, CSPA, 1984. The principles of strategic planning and management, properly adapted and implemented, can bring greater coherence and effectiveness to government. The book presents an approach to strategic planning and management broad enough to be applicable to the widely varying circumstances of individual state and local governments. $11.95.

The Wealth of States: Policies for a Dynamic Economy, Roger Vaughn, Robert Pollard and Barbara Dyer, CSPA, 1985. The Wealth of States presents a framework for development policy and examines practical steps states can take to implement this new agenda. The ideas presented stem from the notion that economic development is a process of change and adaption to change. Innovation — new ideas, products and processs — is the fuel and entrepreneurs are the engine of development. $16.95

The Learning Enterprise: Adult Learning, Human Capital and Economic Development, Lewis J. Perlman, CSPA, 1984. The recent frenzy over elementary and secondary education has obscured an adult learning crisis that puts the U.S. economy "at risk". The author argues that human capital in the post industrial age requires a new kind of learning enterprise — focused on adults rather than children, on the process of technology of learning rather than education institutions, and on private competition rather than publica administration. $10.00

Preventing Teenage Pregnancy: A Public Policy Guide, Susan Foster, CSPA, 1986. The U.S. has by far the highest rate of teenage pregnancy of any industrial society. The result is enormous numbers of abortions, severe health risks, school dropouts, diminished job prospects, troubled youngsters and reliance on public assistance. But it is, the author contends, "a preventable social problem." $11.95